'CRY'

The Tears of The Girl from Birkenhead

By Trish Ollman

Disclaimer: Some names and Identifying details have been changed in 'CRY' to protect the privacy of individuals.

Copyright 2020 Trish Ollman

Also by Trish Ollman

A Girl from Birkenhead
Dear Alice
Escape to Paradise Island
Return to Paradise Island
The Office Girls
Last Resort (Screenplay)
'ANNIE' (Screenplay)
'CRY'

Books available from Amazon (Worldwide)

Website: www.trishollmanauthor.com

This book is dedicated to my only daughter, who has supported me throughout my journey and given me the courage to write this book.

CRY

THE CHILDHOOD YEARS

Have you ever had a memory from years ago that you hadn't previously thought about since? A memory, or memories, that will maybe, and possibly would, affect the rest of your life? Well that has happened to me. In my first attempt at writing my Autobiography, I was so anxious to get it, my first ever book, published, that I just wrote of things that immediately sprang to mind, nothing 'personal', almost just an 'outline' of my life. Now almost five years later, I realize just how much I had left out of that small first book, 'A Girl from Birkenhead'. I've recently been told that it's cathartic to meet trauma head-on, so that's what I intend to do in this sequel to 'A Girl from Birkenhead', 'CRY', as that is what I have been doing for almost all of my life. For those of you who have read the first book, there will be some parts of my life that you will already know, however, this will be a 'no holds barred' account of the real life of myself. A Girl from Birkenhead!

I was born Patricia Ann Walsh on 29th July 1952, to parents John and Hilda Walsh, in Grange Mount Maternity Hospital in Birkenhead, Cheshire, in the United Kingdom, which, at the time, was a very poor part of the Country. I never really knew my father's parents, as they had died when I was very small, but my grandma, Bertha Davies, and grandad Bill, were to become, for eleven years at least, my saviors. My Dad's father came from County Cork, in Ireland, and it was during the Irish Civil War that Grandad John (Jack) Walsh had to flee the Country. This would have been around 1922, and, as he had a 'price' put on his head, as he had become a Gun Runner, so he had to hot-foot it by boat, over the Irish Sea, to Liverpool in England. It was there that he met a lovely young Englishwoman called Gertrude (or Gertie) Beresford. She had grown up in Southern England but had come to the Liverpool area to become a housemaid. John (or Jack, as he was known) married Gertie, settling in Birkenhead, were they went on to have 3 children, my Dad being the baby of the family. Mum's family were mostly English and Welsh, although it was to my horror that I found out a few years ago, that my great, great Grandfather on my Mum's side, had emigrated to England from Germany. Having spent a lot of time with Grandma, who had lived through the War, I suppose my hatred of Germans, (I don't have it now: I have met some lovely German people whilst selling my Books) must have come from that time. For many years, I would watch Films and Documentaries of the Nazi Regime and the horror of it all, so I supposed being brought up in the late 50s, and with my Grandparents who had lived through it, it's not surprising that I felt like I did.

As far as I know, my Grandad's family had come from Wales, as their name was Davies, and we can place my grandad's family in North Wales on an Ancestry

CRY

Site. So, my time spent with my maternal Grandparents, at weekends and in the school holidays, made parts of that stage of my life bearable. However, when thy had both died in 1963 and '64 respectively, all eight of us, (six children and my parents) moved into their small two-up, two-down terrace house in the town of Birkenhead, which lies across the River Mersey from Liverpool, home of the famous Beatles. If nothing else, my parents were prolific in childbearing. Following me, in 1953 my brother David was born, then in 1955, Peter, Anne followed in 1957, and Linda in 1959. After a break, the sixth and last child, Diane, was born in 1964. I remember that she was named after the Frank Ifield song, 'Smile for Me, My Diane'. My mother had never actually learnt how to be a 'mother' to her children, and it certainly wasn't instinctive. She herself had grown up in that same house in Cardigan Street with Grandma and Grandad, and with a brother, William (Bill), and a sister, Edna, who were both older. She had lived there until she had become pregnant with me, then marrying my Dad (John Walsh) at the young age of just nineteen. My grandparents were lovely, kind and gentle people, but although I felt happy there, and was looked after so much better than at home, they too were unable to show affection. I can say now that I FELT affection, especially from Grandma, but neither she nor grandad would offer a touch or a kiss, and certainly there would be no "I Love You". I would spend time with them until they died when I was eleven and twelve, In the summer school holidays,

TRISH OLLMAN

Grandma and Grandad took me, along with Aunty Annie, my Grandma's sister who had lived next door all her life, on day trips with Harding's Coaches, to 'far away' places, such as Blackpool, Southport and Rhyl in North Wales. Just going through the Mersey Tunnel (which links Birkenhead and the Wirral with Liverpool) was exciting in itself, as we rarely did it. To be able to drive under a large River inside a tunnel, which was lit only with low voltage lighting (it had a smell, a kind of petrol or diesel, that I can still smell to this day!) was cause for much excitement, even though we lived no more than five minutes away from it.

I have no memories from before I was about five. When it was time for me to start school, my Dad, a staunch Catholic (my Mum was Church of England) took me to the top of the street and asked me if I wanted to go to that 'horrible' (C. of E.) school to the left, or to a 'lovely' school (Catholic, of course), to the right. Naturally I chose the lovely school on the right. I sat on the handlebars of his pushbike, and away we went. One of only a few memories I have of my first day at St Albans Roman Catholic School, in Wallasey, Cheshire, was of sitting in another child's seat, because there were crayons and paper on their desk, whereas my new desk had nothing on it. I certainly didn't cry, it was just another part of life, and even at that young age, I had no emotional or physical connection to either of my parents. My brother, David, a year younger than me, was very jealous that I got to go to school, and would whine every morning to be

CRY

allowed to go with me. The only other memory of those early weeks at St Albans was of a collection tin for the 'poor children' being passed around the class. I have no idea how it came about, but I told my teacher that I had put a sixpenny piece into that tin, but when she checked, there was no sixpenny piece in there, so I was sent to the Headmistress's office for lying. I wish I could remember what punishment, if any, I was given, but I can't. Neither can I remember why on earth I would have said that I had put the sixpence in when I didn't!

My brother, David, joined me there the following year. Again, I have little or no memories of that time, other than one day, David and I went into St Albans church next to our school and lit a candle each to 'Our Lady' (you were supposed to pay a penny for each candle you lit, but we didn't). Obviously, we couldn't pay (where would we have got a penny from!) and it was unfortunate that standing behind us as we perpetrated this heinous crime, was the Headmistress of our school, a stern Nun. That was the first (and would be only one of two canings I ever received) time that I 'got the cane' – a kind of thin walking stick struck with some force across our open hands. Again, I didn't cry and neither did my brother. In fact, if I remember rightly, we actually laughed about it after leaving the Headmistresses office. Our school was a bus ride away, with the bus fare being a penny. We didn't always get the penny but on the days that we did, David and I would walk to school and spend the penny on sweets – Black Jacks and Fruit Salad, or Milk Chews (4 for a penny) being our favorites. I imagine my next brother, Peter, would have started school the following year, but I have no memory of it. I do remember that we were all transferred to another school, St Joseph's Roman Catholic school, also in Wallasey, (I think our parents were politely asked to move us to another school!) but apart from having to stand out in front of the class with a group of other kids, and recite The Lord's Prayer in Latin (I 'mouthed' the words incorrectly, with the group, as I didn't know it – "Stand in the corner, Pat Walsh!" – the rest of my time at that school is a blank, although I did make my first Holy Communion when I was there. I can remember a white dress (I used the picture that was taken on that day for the front cover of 'A Girl from Birkenhead', one of only two photos I have of my childhood).

The first house I remember us living in was in Roker Avenue, Wallasey, (Cheshire). It was a three-bedroom semi-detached brick house with a red tiled roof and a big back garden. We had a dog called Monty and a bird called Pip. The bird would sit on our shoulder and we would feed it bits of bacon rind. (Somewhere along the way, I developed a really bad fear of birds, a phobia, especially when they fly near me. No idea when, how or why!). We found out that our dog, Monty, was not a boy as we'd thought, but a girl, so Mum changed her name to Montina. My Dad worked at The National Coal Board as a Clerk but his wages must

CRY

have been low because there was never enough money to go around from payday to payday, and my Mum was what most mothers were back then, a housewife. So far so good. No other memories come to mind. However, it's around this time that I do remember. I would have been about seven years old (probably about 1959), and if one of us children got sick with mumps, measles or chickenpox (all very prevalent at the time) then that sick child would have to sleep downstairs in the 'front room' – a room that was used for no other purpose, none that we kids ever knew of anyway, as my parents never entertained. Where would they have got the money from for a bottle of wine when they couldn't even afford a pint of fresh milk? (We only ever had 'Milk Powder' which my Dad would make in a jug with water as weakly as possible to make the powder in the tin last longer!) There was a 'bed settee' (a sofa bed) and very little other furniture in the 'lounge'. It was my time to sleep downstairs, as I had, I think, the mumps, and was banished to that 'front room' with its bed settee. What followed was to leave the rest of my childhood, except for a few other more memorable moments, both with, and without my lovely grandparents (they had both died by the time I was twelve) in a dark, dark blackness of nothingness. What I do remember is that I was laying on my left side on the bed settee, it was daylight, I remember, as the sun was shining in through the partly-drawn curtains sending long shadows across my fawn blanket. (I find it amazing that I can remember the color. Suddenly, my next memory is of my dad getting into the bed next to me and I felt something hard sticking into my back. (I now know that it was his erect penis). I froze. Naturally I knew nothing at all about sex, or about any kind of intimacy at all, why would I at such a young age, as both my parents, right throughout their lives, never did, or would, ever show any of their six children any signs of love or affection. There was no touching, no words of kindness, praise or encouragement. Nothing. With six children and only one small wage coming into our two-up, two-down terraced house, I can now, with hindsight, realize that a) they should never had had six children, and b) that they were probably trying to just get through life the best they could.

So back to 1959, I was 'frozen' when my dad had got into bed with me. Luckily, I don't remember mush else, other than his hand touching me in a place where he shouldn't have done, and the hard thing sticking into my young back. I instinctively knew that my Dad had done a bad thing, but didn't know what to do with the information. I wasn't close to my cruel and aggressive mother, nor, at that time, my brothers, so the last thing I would even think of doing was telling anyone. And I was only seven. Late that day, and daily until I was about 17 or 18 at various times, I would get a kind of 'buzzing' song running through my head, without warning or at various times, I would get a kind of 'buzzing' song running through my head, without warning or event. Another time, as he continued with his sexual abuse, I was alone in my bedroom, and my

CRY

Dad came in, then took out his penis, and tried to put it in my mouth, grabbing me by the back of the head, and all done without a single word being spoken. Even at such a young age, I knew this wasn't right and I pushed him away and ran out of the room, and downstairs. My Dad must have had great faith in me that I wouldn't tell on him and I wonder where he got that knowledge from? And that's it. Apart from my few memories of those lovely days out with my grandma, I remember barely nothing, the years following that day up until I was in my teens, and I only remember a black nothingness (I've since found out this is common amongst abused children) mostly just one big black hole, although I do have the memory of my parents buying or renting a Fish and Chip shop when I was nine. The shop itself was directly opposite another Chip Shop, 'Wilfs', and was in Rawson Road, Seaforth, Liverpool, the only time we ever lived on that side of the River Mersey. The shop itself had been closed for a while and on our first day there, there was a little freezer in the empty shop that contained ice creams that had all melted and stuck together. We kids were allowed to eat them as best we could, but boy, were they a treat, as the freezer was half full of them, all stuck together.

I received a nasty injury whilst we had lived in that Chip Shop. (We were only there about a year and had to close down, as 'Wilf's' had a good, regular customer base, and had been there for years, I think.) My brother David had taken off somewhere with my Dad's garden spade (Why did we need a spade when we had no garden, no grass – another of life's mysteries!) and I had been sent to find him and tell him to get home. I found him soon enough and as we walked back to the Chip Shop (we lived above it) somehow the spade cut through the Achilles tendons in my heel. (I've no idea if David did it on purpose or not!) I fell to the ground and there was soon a small group of other, curious, kids standing around me. My ankle was bleeding heavily I tried to stand up but couldn't, so I sent one of the girls to the Chip Shop, which was only on the next block, to fetch my Mum. The girl soon returned and told me "Your Mum said to get back home, now!" But when I tried to stand up again, I couldn't, and the pain in my heel was excruciating. Unfortunately, what I didn't know then, and wasn't to know for quite a few months, was that the spade had severed the Achilles tendons in my heel. The same girl went back to tell my Mum that I couldn't stand up, but I can imagine my now very frustrated mother smoldering with anger. She marched down to where I was still laying on the pavement, and 'ordered' me to get up and "get home now", so with the help of David and another girl, I had to hop, blood pouring from my wound, back home. I think you may now get some idea of what a great Mum I had, hey! My ankle was bandaged and I was sent to school the following day as usual, But I could barely walk, and my right foot was turned out at a 90% angle at the ankle. Mum told my teacher to "hit my leg with the ruler" if I didn't walk with my foot straight, so for quite a few months, I

CRY

would receive a smack or the ruler whenever either my Mum or one of the more meaner teachers saw me and my crooked foot turned out. After a while, and I have no idea how this came about, but Mum took me to Walton Hospital in Liverpool for physiotherapy to correct my foot. It was while we were waiting, that a nurse came in and told us that there was a Doctor who wanted to see me. When I was asked to walk to the end of his office, he immediately said that I had severed the Achilles Tendons. I only remember being in a hospital ward with all 'old' ladies, and having my first operation, where my Tendons were repaired (That repair was to last me forty years before I had to have my Achilles repaired again.) I was in a wheelchair for about three months and crutches for a further six. On the day it happened, our David got a real thrashing from my Dad. Funny, hey, how he could sometimes stick up for me, his plaything? Like my two sisters, I have a black 'nothingness' of my life, in general. The odd memory of importance, yes, but there is generally, just a great big 'nothingness' about my life, nothingness of any loving or an emotional nature. I wonder if that's because none of us ever received either one?

When the Chip Shop went bust, we moved back to Wallasey, to a rented house in Crescent Road. Yet another change of school for me. (You must remember that every school I ever attended, I never had any part of the uniform, and was always a laughing stock to the other kids there, the only one without a uniform.

TRISH OLLMAN

Needless to say, I never made many friends!!) There was a Crisp Factory on the corner of the next road past our house, and it was there that a Revolution was made: they produced the first cheese and onion crisps (up until then, you could only get plain crisps, some with a little blue paper twist of salt hidden deep inside in the depths, (but what fun you could have finding it!) but when you did manage to locate it, you had the extra pleasure if sprinkling the salt over the crisps, then shaking the bag to evenly coat them all. (Gee, such simple entertainment that was had by us Walsh kids!) David and I would walk home from school to save the bus fare, and buy a halfpenny's worth of the scraps which the manufacturers would keep for us every Friday. They were put in a brown paper bag for us, and to this day, my favorite thing to eat would be the scraps from the bottom of a packet of cheese and onion crisps! One very early morning when we were at Crescent Road, (it was still dark), I was woken by my brother, David, who was crying and telling me that my grandma had died. I went downstairs with him, where Mum was making a pan of porridge to feed us all before we went to grandma's house. Being so poor, we couldn't afford the bus fare for us all to make the journey from Wallasey to my grandparent's house in Cardigan Street, which is just off Conway Street, a major road through the main part of Birkenhead town. Being November (1963) it was a freezing cold day and Mum, even though my grandfather, her Dad, had cycled over the 'Four Bridges' from Birkenhead to us in Wallasey, (it would have been a good half hour ride for

CRY

him, knowing that his wife of 40 years or so, was lying dead in her bed back home - No phone's back then for him to inform his children that their Mum had died.) So my poor, poor grandad had to make the arduous journey on his old pushbike, not only to tell us, but also to tell his other two children and their families, all who lived in either Birkenhead or Wallasey. So even though I might have little good to say about my Mum when I was a child, I admire her enormously for making that pan of porridge before leaving to go to her parent's house and say her goodbyes to her Mum, who at only 63 years of age, had died of pneumonia. Grandma was my savior, even if only for a short time in my life, and I can never thank her enough for the love, care, and normality she gave to me. Bertha Osterman-Davies. RIP. Until we meet again!

Arriving at Cardigan Street, all of us kids were told to wait outside the house. Then one by one, we were taken through to the little living room where grandma had her bed (She hadn't slept upstairs in years, she'd once told me!) All I remember is that half of grandma's face was a dark blue, almost black, and she had no pillow, her head lying flat on the bed. I found that aspect of seeing my beloved grandma dead to be the worst. Where was her pillow? She should have a pillow, I wanted to shout out. (To this day, I feel claustrophobic at the very thought of sleeping flat on a bed, with no pillow!) With all of my siblings, along with my Mum, around me, I realized that I, the child who had been the closest to her, and the only one of her 10 grandchildren whom she had doted on, was not crying. I couldn't. I was probably numb with shock and horror, but I really don't know why I wasn't. I just remember the others all crying around me, and me standing like a statue. It was the first time I had seen someone dead (and would go on to only see another three people who were dead in my life, to date.) All of us children were eventually sent to stand outside in the back yard while the Funeral Home arrived to take Grandma's body away. When we went back in, there was grandma's bed. Empty. We never went to her funeral and I have no other memory of that time, other than my grandad dying almost a year to the day, afterwards, Mum telling us that it was from a 'broken heart' but it was actually lung cancer.

During those years, when we reached the end of Primary School, we had to take the 'Eleven Plus" exam. Your results determined the type of High School you went to. I think there were three levels: A Grammar School, A Middle sort of School, and a School for the Dunces! Luckily, I wasn't a Dunce, but neither was I Mr. Einstein either, so I was sent to Quarry Mount School in Wallasey (where we were living at the time, until grandad died in 1964) I have absolutely no memories from the three months or so that I was at Quarry Mount, other than that on my first day in class there, I accidently fell off my chair, and my teacher immediately labelled me 'The Class Clown'. Luckily, I wasn't there long enough to prove that I actually wasn't a class clown, or a clown of any

CRY

description. Even as unhappy as I was, I would never have dreamt of putting on a 'happy face'. At home, there remained a 'black 'hole' of my life. Whilst I don't remember any more of my father's abuse, (I started to have 'flashbacks' when I was in my thirties, and remembered a lot when I saw a Psychiatrist, but more on that later.) I just have a big, black hole in my life, at home, and especially about my Dad. Sure, he was always around, but everything else eludes me. (It is amazing that my other two sisters also have 'black holes' in their memories of their lives as children growing up!) My Mum, Hilda, had she have been the right age and born much earlier than 1933, could have easily been re-incarnated as a member of the Gestapo, such was her mental and physical cruelty. My two brothers and I just accepted it, as we knew no better. (It wasn't until much later in life that we were to realize that there were some children who actually did have loving, caring parents. But unfortunately for us, we were not part of that group.) She liked to use her finger nails and dig them into my arm and draw blood, that was when we were out of the house, in view of people. She could then do it slyly so as not to be seen. At home, her favorite form of entertainment was to pull my head down (I had shoulder length hair) and knee me in the face, causing bleeding on many occasions. Another favorite was hitting me and my two brothers with either a wire coat hanger, my Dad's belt (buckle-end, of course!) or the big bread knife, sometimes holding it by the handle, other times by the silver blade. (Although sometimes my Dad would also partake in this pleasure!) I wasn't alone in her beatings, David and Peter would also receive similar treatment, but I think she may have had a deep-rooted resentment of me, particularly, as I had always been her Mum's (my Grandma's) 'favorite. Still, a beating's a beating, but, hey, didn't every kid's Mum do that to their kids?

After grandad had died in November 1964, all eight of us moved into 20 Cardigan Street (Birkenhead), where my beloved grandma had lived since her marriage to grandad. (She was born in 1900, and brought up, next door, at number 22, until she married, then moved next door.) The house was a late Victorian brick terrace, very typical of its day, with 2 bedrooms and a tiny 'Box Room' upstairs, a 'Parlor' room in the front of the house – never used (again, WHY with such a big family?), which housed a settee, an old piano (My Dad could play – and would go on to play in a Pub in Bromborough when he was much older) but for reasons unknown, he never played it for us. Ever! There was also an old-fashioned record player and some thick black records (I think they were called 33's but I could be wrong!) Again, they were never played for us. Ever. So that room remained unused. (No bed settee/couch for 'sick' kids by this time.) The only other main room was 'The Living Room'. All eight of us, six kids and two parents lived all of their daily lives in that one small room. We had a three-seater couch, a single old armchair, (most of us kids sat on the floor), a sideboard (I can remember that there were two small

CRY

black ivory elephants on it and they had belonged, as had a lot of other things in the house, to my grandparents before they died.) and, amazingly for parents who couldn't even send their children to school in any semblance of uniform, we had a Rediffusion small black and white TV. (The tall Rediffusion antenna mast was located in the street behind and towered above us.) It sat on a little single door cupboard that, for some odd reason, was full of old shoes. One day, when Mum was out and Dad at work at Cammel Laird's Shipbuilders – Four generations of my family had worked there at some point – I put all the old odd shoes into a bag, (most didn't even have a match), and I sent our David to the Pawn Shop on the corner of Exmouth Street (Birkenhead) and gave him a hand-written note, supposedly from my Mum, asking the Pawnbroker if he could 'loan' us ten shillings on this bag of old shoes. What do you reckon? Did he come back with the ten bob? I remember being quite disappointed! I had been looking forward to a bag of chips. No idea what the pawn broker's problem was. The shoes may have been 'odd' but they were still Ok – just!!

The only other room downstairs was a tiny kitchen. We had a gas stove and a sink. It was in this stone sink that all six children (and Mum & Dad, assumingly) would have an 'all-over wash' every Friday, (with Lifebuoy Soap, if we had any!) On the wall was a very small cupboard with wire mesh on the front. This was our 'food cupboard'. It consisted of flour, salt, sugar (sometimes), powdered milk, and a box containing various quantities, depending on when pay day was, of Cornflakes. On the floor by the cupboard was always a large bag of potatoes. Every night of the week, either myself, our David or Mum (depending on her mood) would make 2 lots of home-made chips in a chip pan full of melted lard, on the gas stove. Being the eldest, I was always a 'second batch' kid, and would often be so hungry that I would pinch one of the 'first batch' kid's chips. Often, there might be a fried egg, or a spoonful of baked beans (When I first met my future husband Mike, the first time I went around to his place, as an only child, he greatly impressed me by having A WHOLE tin of beans to himself (unheard of!!) and not one, but two pieces of toast! He also took a BOTTLE of real milk out of their small fridge (first time I ever saw a fridge), took the silver top off it, and drank from the bottle! Surely this was the most rich and exotic boy I could ever have found!! Hmmmm) Still, I digress. So, in OUR little food cupboard, even we could boast something that even Mike and his fancy little fridge didn't have. Wait for it… we had a PADLOCK on our cupboard, a padlock that only had 2 keys: one each for Mum and Dad. Surely, naughty children shouldn't be allowed free access to all the goodies in our cupboard? Imagine what we could have made with all that salt and powdered milk, even better if there was a bit of sugar! One evening, when, for some reason, Mum and Dad went out (they never did, so no idea why they went to!) Me, David and Peter (the three younger girls were all in bed) were so hungry that our

CRY

David devised a way of opening the Golden Gate to our food cupboard. With the edge of a knife, he prized the metal lattice-work off the front at the corner, a space just big enough for his hand to reach in, and, egged on by Peter and I, managed to pull out the small bit of sugar that was in there. I added some of the sugar (not too much as we would have gotten a hiding if found out) to some water in, of all things, a roasting tin. I then boiled this up, but hark! Was that a key opening the front door? Yes. Our parents were back. I quickly grabbed the hot tin with a tea towel and shoved the lot under the couch. I have no idea why Mum didn't miss that tin, but I bet her face was a picture many months later, when a nasty smell was coming from the vicinity of the couch (don't forget, it was also her bed!). I never knew that green mold mixed with just sugar and water would smell? Would you?

THE EARLY TEEN YEARS

At the age of 12, and now living in my grandparent's house after they had both died, to say that the 8 of us living in such a tiny house, all squashed in together, is quite an understatement! The 2 boys shared the small box room (how on earth did they fit 2 beds in there? Maybe we lived in a 16-room mansion and I'm, remembering it all wrong!! Don't think so!) We 4 girls all slept in the front bedroom, and my Dad had the middle room, just a few meters away from the door of the girls' room. My bed was completely in eye-line with the door (which we were never allowed to close). As I said earlier, a lot of what had happened with my Dad only really came back to me when I was a lot older but it is at this time (I would have been around aged 12) that I have the most vivid memories of him come back. (All of the other memories I have from when I was a bit older are much deeper, and some forgotten, even today). But what I do remember consisted of him touching me and rubbing his bare penis up against me. To understand better, you need to know that the other 3 girl's beds were placed along 2 walls away from the door of our room. Unfortunately, my bed ran parallel to the door, the head in direct line with the open door, and Dad always insisted it was to be kept open (I wonder why? As was usual, I never questioned it. Each night, he would come up to bed while I was always still awake (Mum would be downstairs, as usual on the couch: No more babies for her!!) My Dad would make sure the landing light was on, shining bright above his head, always, and without going into his bedroom, standing outside his room on the landing, he would, with complete knowledge, standing in plain view of me so that I would see him, he would slowly undress completely, then 'play' with himself, flicking hid long penis up and down. He would, after a few minutes, then masturbate, still standing outside of his bedroom, and knowing full well that I could see him. Why didn't I tell my Mum? Why didn't I tell my teacher? Why? I have no idea. I have no explanation. I didn't even tell my brother David, who was the closest of my

CRY

siblings to me. It has been suggested to me that as it was just a continuation of the sexual abuse I'd had since aged seven, I would not have been able to make anything abnormal about it, or, I might have thought it was a normal thing for him to do. Maybe all Dads did it to their oldest daughters. Sounds ridicules as I write it now, but... I have no explanation as to why I let this go on for about three years, that I can remember, anyway. It wasn't to be until I became older that I started to realize the significance of what he had done, and was still doing. I knew it was wrong. I thought that maybe, other girls Dad's didn't do that to them, but I couldn't be sure and it was never spoken about. Had my Mum been a 'real Mum' maybe I could have told her. But she wasn't, so I didn't.

Some memories of other parts of my life do start to come back from around this time. My grandma had died so I had no 'support', if you know what I mean? Myself, as well as my 2 brothers, were to bear the brunt of our Mum's increasing physical and emotional abuse. (I can't really remember much of my three young sisters at this time, but maybe they experienced similar behavior after I had left home? I don't know) We were used to the beatings, the belt, the coat hanger, the bread knife, her nails scratching deep into my arms, but this was where the emotional abuse from her really hit its straps. When we'd moved to Cardigan Street, I was sent to Conway Street school, a large red brick Victorian building in the Centre of Birkenhead (the building still stands today), about a four to five-minute walk from home) It was an All Girls' school and, like every other school in the Country, the pupils were expected to wear the correct uniform. For the pupils at Conway Street, of which I was to be one. The uniform was a straight navy blue skirt, white blouse, and a navy V-neck jumper. White ankle socks and black shoes were worn by every girl. They all had the 'uniform'. Except me. My 'uniform', was one of two old dresses I'd had for about two years, Mum had sold what little bits of 'uniform' (Isn't it unbelievable what you could sell back in the day? Imagine trying to sell a second-hand, well-worn pair of bright red and white diamond-pattered socks on eBay nowadays?) I had had at my previous school. I had been given those dresses by my Auntie Pat, who cousin Pauline had grown out of at the time. They were classed by me as 'old-fashioned' dresses (Don't forget this was the 60's, not quite yet 'Flower Power", but definitely the Beatles era and the start of a new Teen Movement that would change the world into the next Century, and beyond, and I really just wanted to be like all other modern teenagers) Plus the fact that these dresses were getting too tight for me. Telling my Mum that I absolutely HAD to have the uniform, she once again said she couldn't afford it but she would (begrudgingly) go to the Market next week and try and get me another dress. Telling her I HAD to have the uniform fell on deaf ears (as it was to fall for my sisters in later years. The annoying part of this saga was that she probably COULDN'T afford a new uniform for me, but she COULD afford the quarter of Sugared Almonds every

CRY

few days – which she kept 'hidden and safeguarded" in her handbag. She could also afford to smoke, probably at least a pack a day, as did my Dad, and, so cruel to us kids. as we hated the fatty taste of Stork margarine, along with the Sugared Almonds safely tucked away in her handbag, there would always be a pack of 'Lurpak Best Butter which only she could have. Us kids, and I assume my Dad, used 'Stork' cooking margarine for our bread and toast, but Mum could somehow 'Afford" the more than double 'Best Butter' for herself. So, by now my dresses were getting too tight for me, and they were really washed-out and scruffy, and I wondered what dress Mum would find at the market for me the following week. Next Saturday, coming home from the market (Why not take me with her to choose?) she must have thought I was still nine, as the dress she'd bought had little flowers all over it, was canary yellow and just fitted. Just. I suppose if you squinted (a lot) or wore glasses with thick, thick lenses, the dress COULD have looked like a white blouse and navy skirt, probably not but who cared! ME!!! So all of my dresses were now getting too tight for me, and as my body was developing, and along with a few other old bits and pieces that I had that barely fit, I had my 'Uniform' and again, was the laughing stock of the school. As if the clothes weren't bad enough, I also had to wear whatever manky old shoes my Mum could find. I can remember going at least a whole term with, not the short white ankle socks of the other girls' uniform, no, not for me, but a pair of knee-high bright red and white 'diamond' patterned socks. The only girl in a school of around 500 girls with different socks. For many weeks, I can remember that every time I arrived in the playground before school, there would be dozens of girls laughing at me and pointing. But I suppose that they soon got tired of it, and moved onto something else. But I would forever be 'The Odd one'! One day, during the morning at school, one of my old shoes broke – the sole came away from the shoe. I had no option but to miss my FREE school dinner (the only decent meal we ever got was at school) and to walk home shoeless where my angry Mum had no option but to give me sixpence (she gave it very begrudgingly) to try and buy another manky old pair from the second-hand shoe shop in Exmouth Street. The shop itself was dark and dingy, and was run by 2 women, a mother and daughter I think. (The old lady would be sitting in the back, almost in the dark) There were 3 trestle tables, one along each wall, and each one was piled high with, mostly, odd shoes. Now this was the mid 1960's the days of The Beatles and on the fringes and 'modern' clothes and shoes, not 'whatever you can find that a) fit, and b) you can find the other shoe that matched it. Often, the old lady would be summonsed from her chair in the dark, to help us try and 'find' the other matching shoe, if indeed I did, find a shoe that was modern enough, and fit me. One day, the 'modern' pair that I could find that actually fit, were a pair of pointed toe, white high heels. What possessed me, a 12-or-13-year-old schoolgirl, to hand over my sixpence for them, then try and walk back to school in them, I will never know.

CRY

Well, it doesn't matter, because I didn't. I couldn't. You try walking in a pair of pointed-toe white high heels, with a pair of knee-high red and white diamond-patterned socks on. You just wouldn't, would you? So, half way back to school, and who should be walking towards me, with our Diane in her pram, but my lovely Mum!! She looked. Shook her head and looked again. I was grabbed by the hair (Shoulder length for ease of inflicting the greatest amount of pain!) and told to "Take those bloody things back, NOW!". Only problem was, the woman who ran the shop wouldn't give me my sixpence back and was very reluctant to let me exchange them. So, after yet another solid half hour searching for something else that fit. I left the shop in a pair of – horror of horrors – old brown men's brogues, the only shoe that fit my big size 9 feet, and the only shoe in which we could find its mate. And to add insult to injury, they didn't even have shoe laces. Luckily the older lady once again came out of the back to face a, by now, crying me, and pulled 2 black shoelaces from 2 other odd shoes. And THAT is how I arrived back at school, about an hour late. Sounds a bit 'far-fetched' hey? But no, it's all true. I was to return to that shop a number of times over the next 3-4 years, all with a similar result.

It was also when I was about 12, and we had moved into Grandma's house in Cardigan Street, that there was a kind of religious 'Hall' at the top of the street, on Hemmingford Street, (there was also a school on that street where Mike went to; Hemmingford Street Boys

School, which later became Hamilton Secondary School, and a stone's throw away from my own school in Conway Street, but I was unaware of him at that time) This Hall was called 'Thompson's Mission' and my only knowledge of it was that twice a week, myself and my siblings, apart from Diane, who was still too young, would attend. Thursdays, after singing a few children's hymns ("Jesus Loves the Little Children, all the Children of the World. Red and Yellow, Black and White, they are precious in His sight, Jesus Loves the Little Children of the World!") we would stand in line and receive a somewhat stale fruit bun. Most of the other kids, especially the boys, would use these buns to throw at one another, and use as 'weapons – they were that hard! But us Walshes? No way would we waste a stale fruit bun, and we would gobble it down before making our way back home, 2 minutes away. Then every Sunday, we would go again. There was a large stage at the front, and this would contain various items which we children could pick one from at the end of the Service. These items, some books and old toys, a few clothes and the odd pair of shoes, had obviously been donated to Thompsons Mission, but by whom, I have no idea. However, this was to be my siblings and my first opportunity to get some items for ourselves, as we had previously had very little in the way of possessions prior to now. Sometimes, if one of us found an item of ANY value, Mum would sell it before we had had a chance to use or play with it, or wear it! I remember we would feel the loss of something we'd managed to get from the mission if Mum did take it off

CRY

us to sell, or sometimes, if suitable, for herself. One time, when I was there one Sunday, as we were making our way to a pew, I spotted the Holy of Holy's: a pair of white pointed toe shoes with a small heel. Now, I remembered the fuss Mum had made over those high-heeled shoes from Exmouth Street Shoe Shop not that long ago, however, these shoes had only a small pointed heal. I desired those shoes like I had desired nothing else and they HAD to be mine. As there were a number of other teenage girls at the mission, I had to make sure that I was the girl who got those shoes. Once we had said our prayers and sang a few hymns, I got up and rushed to the front of the queue. Yes, I got them, and the feeling of success was a new experience for me. I had no socks on and only dirty white plimpsoles (pumps). I immediately put them on and tottered home. My Mum went mad when she saw them and I got the belting around the head that she found so satisfying. "Get them back right now!" Yet again, and I still wonder to this day, what on earth could have been wrong with a 13-year old wearing a shoe with a little heel, although even I now admit, it really was a 'woman's' shoe. So, crying, (I so desperately wanted to be modern and like all the others girls of that time!) I now had the indignity of taking the shoes back to Thompson's Mission. They were starting to pack away when I arrived, and the only things left on the stage was a thin book or a jigsaw. I chose the book. Little did I know then that this act alone would bring me many, many years pleasure and allow me to escape my life for a short while, at least. That book? It was an Agatha Christie, (Can't remember which one) but it was to become the start of my love affair with her books. Over the course of my life, I have, four or five times, collected all 77 of her books. (I always ended up having to sell them when we needed the money, but that's later! I was also privileged to visit Agatha's house Greenway, in Devon not that long ago, where I cried with joy at knowing my heroine had once walked these very halls, and lived in these very rooms. I was allowed to sit at her piano and even sat on her toilet – The National Trust will let you do that!)

It was while I was going to Thompson's Mission, that I was to become sexually active. I still have that 'black hole' at this point, about my Dad, but I do remember him at this time being very abusive towards us all, joining my Mum. One of the boys, Tommy Becall, had been coming to Thompson's Mission for a while, and he was always paying me compliments, telling me how pretty I was etc. So when he asked me to 'go out' with him, naturally I agreed. He took me to his house, and I remember there were no Adults there, only another boy of about 14. Tommy himself would have been slightly older, about 16 maybe? It soon became apparent that I was there for only one reason. Tommy led me to a bunk bed and had sex with a stone statue, ME. There were no words spoken, and no 'foreplay' (not that I'd have wanted it) But afterwards, Tommy then he got his friend (no idea who the other boy was) to also have a go. It was obviously the younger boy's

CRY

first time, as I can remember him being very nervous. It was soon over and for some obscure reason, I cooked mince and mashed potato for the three of us. The fact that I had felt not a single thing during the sex didn't even enter my head. Girls were not meant to moan and groan, or even enjoy, sex as the boys did. It was easy for us girls. All we had to do was just lay there! Easiest job in the world! I never saw Tommy or his friend again. But I now had to go home and face the wrath of my Mum for being out all afternoon.

A year later, and I turned 13. I'd got my period when I was 11 and had been stealing boxes of Tampax each month from the local supermarket. My Mum knew I had started, but made no effort at all at buying me sanitary products. If for whatever reason I had no Tampax, I would use a sock, newspaper, anything. My Mum never said a word. Don't ask me why, (well I was only 11 onwards and not very mature!) but I would throw the used Tampax or sock under my bed. One day I came home from school and Mum had done the unthinkable. She'd gone upstairs to (I assume) tidy our bedroom, something she never did. Her face was like thunder when I got home. She had found the used things under my bed. Now, I had been hit by her many, many times, and I expected what was to come, but not what she did. She waited until the whole family was home, including my Dad, and marched us all upstairs to see my 'mess'. She then beat me black and blue and warned the other girls that if they ever did the same, this would be what they got. I was kept off school for a week, as my bruised and bloodied face would have alerted the authorities. Not long after that incident, I can't remember his name, or where I met him, but a boy, older than my 13 years, gave me some compliment or other (I think it was about my hair, which in those days, was thick and shiny - No idea why, as we never used shampoo, only Lifebuoy Soap, although that was when we had any soap at all!) and asked me to go to the Pictures (Cinema) with him. I had never been out after teatime before so, cunningly, around six, I said I wasn't well, and could I go up to bed. Amazingly, I was allowed to, as this was a first for any of us Walsh kids to actually WANT to go to bed. Upstairs, I brushed my hair (No bathroom in our house – we had a once a week 'all over wash' in the stone kitchen sink, one at a time, with me being the eldest having to wait until last!) and then crept downstairs, along the corridor (the living room door was shut, especially in the colder months, to keep in what little heat our small, round oil heater gave out.) Freedom. It was the first time, apart from going to the shop for groceries, that I had been out by myself. And in the evening as well! I felt grown up and free. I met the boy, let's call him Phil, outside the ABC Cinema in Argyle Street, he paid for us to get in and we sat on the back row. As I sat in my seat, I noticed that there were quite a few other young couples, but they were kissing, and there was one boy who was squeezing a girl's breast. This shocked me as I remember thinking "only Dads can do that" but soon enough, 'Phil' had put his arm around me and tried to kiss me. Without thinking, and

CRY

also without any sort of feeling, physical, emotional or otherwise, I allowed him to. Soon his hand was also squeezing my breast. I didn't particularly like it nor hate it. I just had not one iota of feeling about it, nor the kiss. Now those of you with a weak disposition may care to pass over the next bit (Ha! I bet you don't!) It just so happened that I had my period on that night, and when 'Phil' put his fingers somewhere they shouldn't have been, I felt VERY uncomfortable and mortified with shame. Why didn't I say something to him? I wish I knew. But still I said nothing. I was wracked with embarrassment, as I knew what the end result would be for him. After the Film had ended, 'Phil' said he'd "walk me home". This was all new to me, so I didn't object. But I was very worried about how I would get a good belting once I got home, as I'd snuck out earlier, the first time I have ever done so. On our way home, walking down Market Street, there was a back alley (a narrow passageway which allowed occupants of houses in a street to use the back door via this alleyway.) and 'Phil' pulled me into it. He held me against the wall and, still not realizing in the dark that I had my period, he unzipped his pants, took out his erect penis (nothing new to me. I'd seen my Dad's many times!) and pulled down my school knickers (I only ever had one pair at a time, so imagine how rancid they must have been!) and had sex with me. It was definitely a 'Wham-Bam-Thank-You-Mam' affair and I felt absolutely nothing whatsoever. It wasn't to be until many years later, that I realized that sex for a woman can be as good as it is for a man (although to this day I still wouldn't know! I do know now though, that I had been turned into a block of wood by my Dad's attentions, and would never in my life know of the enjoyment and pleasure that sex can bring to a woman.) After he had finished, 'Phil' said to me "Why didn't you come?" I had no idea what he meant. "Didn't you enjoy it?" Yes, I lied. But did I? Absolutely not. I now know that I had been flattered by him in order for him to get what he wanted from me, a 13-year old girl. (Thinking back, 'Phil' would have been at least 18, if not older!). It wasn't until we reached the now brightly lit Chip Shop, where 'Phil' asked me if I would like to share a bag of chips with him, that he noticed the state of his hands. The only emotion I can remember feeling is shame, as he screamed at me about what a filthy little whore I was. I ran crying all the way home. As that Chip Shop was only a minute or so away from our house, it was our local, and I spent weeks, if not months, dreading my Mum, (or even my brothers if they ever went in there to get my Dad a pie, which they did occasionally) from finding out what I had done. The shame I felt is indescribable. I felt used and dirty. Back at the house, I stood outside our front door for ages, plucking up the courage to knock. (We never had a key) When my Dad finally did open the door, my Mum went berserk and I got a thrashing to end all thrashings. They hadn't even known I'd gone. Had it been worth it? Absolutely not!

That was to be yet another part of my early 'sexual' life. I'd seen plenty of penises in my life. My brothers

CRY

were naturally, much different to my Dad's, and I must say that, even now, so many years later, I have no memory of Dad using his in the same way that 'Phil' did to me, only small 'flashbacks' of what 'did' happen. I don't know why, but to me, sex was no big deal. Naturally, as I got a bit older, I knew enough to be afraid that my parents would find out if I had had sex with a boy, but I can't recall sex ever being something that I should have any emotions about, and I certainly, never once, found the experience to be an exciting or enjoyable one. As life went on for the next 2 years, nothing much changed. Mum and Dad were arguing a bit more, our beltings, sometimes just for talking when we went to bed, continued in the same fashion. The leather belt, the coat hanger, the bread knife, it was all the same to us. We continued to steal sweets (and me, Tampax) from the small supermarket that had recently opened up close by. It was very easy to steal from there as there was only one Assistant, who remained at the till near the door. My brother, Peter, was the most prolific. Chocolate bars were his thing, and often, as I was walking home from school, Peter would be approaching me. As he got close, he would grin and open up his overcoat. There were bars of chocolate everywhere on him. They were down his pants, his socks, and in every pocket of his coat. It's fair play to him that he shared the spoils with David and I. The six children were divided into two groups: Me, David and Peter, who went everywhere together, and my three younger sisters who we knew little about. Surprising really, as all six of us lived in that tiny house in Cardigan Street. I suppose my parents made a bit of an effort every Christmas, but money was very tight, and only one Clerk's wage to give any kind of life to six kids and my parents, must have been hard. But, still I really do think that for that one day, every year, Mum and Dad (well maybe just Mum!) did try to give us a reasonable time. We would all get a couple of small cheap objects, whatever Mum could find, I suppose, and in our stocking (just an old sock on the bottom of our bed) there would be the obligatory tangerine, a few sweets, and if we were lucky, a penny. When I was thirteen, I decided that I wanted to become a hairdresser when I left school. That year, the whole family went on the train, across the River Mersey, to Liverpool. There, were two large stores, Lewises and Blacklers, and both would have a 'grotto'. During my years at Cardigan Street, before I got married, we went twice, once to each store's Grotto. At Lewises, a store with lifts and old men in uniform stopping the lift at each floor, and calling out the name of the goods there. My favorite was "First Floor. Ladies Underwear." For some reason my two brothers and I thought that to be very risqué! The Grotto itself was, even to me at thirteen, a magical place. Us older kids had long since leant about 'Father Christmas' when we found the things we were to get on Christmas Day in Dad's wardrobe! But for some reason, we were very naïve about that Grotto. I think it cost two shillings per child (an awful lot of money for my parents, as there were six children) but for that, as well as a Sleigh Ride, you got to choose a toy or pencil case, or one of an

CRY

assortment of cheap 'tat', as part of your admission price, as well. The 'grotto' was a walk-through area, all curtained off, then you entered a door. Inside was quite a dark room, and in the middle sat a wonderful full-size Sleigh (or some structure that looked like one). When it was full, the room went even darker and the Sleigh would begin to rock. A Christmas tune would be played and the lights crackled on and off. Finally, all the lights came back on and a girl, dressed as an elf, got us all off the Sleigh and out of the door (It was actually another door, but we were so excited that we never noticed!). And then there he was. Father Christmas himself. Sitting on a throne-like chair, a big red nose to match his huge belly and beside him, a wall on which hung 'The Presents Choice'. The younger ones sat on his knee, of course, but my brothers and I were only interested in the presents board. Which to pick? Me being thirteen, David twelve, and Peter eleven, there was not an awful lot of choice, and I think we all three picked a pencil case with two pencils inside, there being nothing else suitable for us teenagers. Still, we were thrilled. All eight of us then went up to "Top Floor. Restaurant" (It was really just a little Café!) where we had two plates of egg and chips between us six kids, while Mum and Dad had a currant bun and a cup of tea. I don't have a lot to thank my parents for, but I did now, as these visits showed us some kind of normality in what were otherwise very unhappy lives. The following year saw us go to Blacklers Store. No lifts or men in uniform there, but instead of a Grotto like Lewises, we had to sit in rows and watch 'The Dancing Waters' – thin spouts of different colored water 'dancing' up and down in time to music. (One of my sisters used to wet the bed and her knickers at the time, and for the rest of the year, me and my brothers called her 'The Dancing Waters'). So that first year, when I decided I wanted to become a hairdresser, I was allowed to choose a small cheap doll for Christmas, something we'd none of us ever been allowed to do before. I chose a pretty little one with almost white, blond nylon hair. I must say that on Christmas Day and for months afterwards that year, I did that poor doll's hair so many times that it ended up falling out. The following year, I decided I wanted to become a writer (!!) and on Christmas morning (I'd already heard Dad come in during the night) there was a large, black, heavy Underwood Typewriter on the bottom of my bed. (I found out many years later that he stole it, hid it under his overcoat, from the office at his work.) It had one of the old-fashioned black and red reel to reel tapes but no paper. I had to wait a few days until Mum could 'blag' some butchers paper, and I eagerly tore it neatly into squares and wrote a few short stories! (No idea what they were, but a budding Writer was in the making!)

For some reason, when I was 14, I was taken out of Conway Street School and sent to St. Winifred's Catholic School. (Conway Street had been C. of E.) I can't remember the exact uniform there (Not that it would have mattered!) but it was an all-girls school again, and there was a tie this time to go with the

CRY

blouse and skirt. I did by this stage have an off-white blouse (it was once white) but no tie. My skirt, instead of the regulation navy blue was actually green and flared. I was told on my first day at St.Winifreds that I MUST have a tie and a blue skirt. The tie was a very thin girls tie (as opposed to the very wide men's ties of the day), and it was grey, blue and red on a diagonal stripe. So, said Mum, of course you must have a tie, oh darling child of mine! She went to Woolworths and did what she did best. She 'improvised'. She came home not with a thin, correctly colored 'girls' tie, but a huge, wide 'man's' tie which was blue (the completely wrong shade of blue mind you) and white, and at least nine inches wide. Ok, so not diagonal stripes, just straight, but "that'll do, won't it?" No Mum. It's too wide and has no red in it and its all wrong! So what does my clever, adaptable Mum do? She gets a red pen out of my pencil case, and DRAWS a red line through the stripes. And that is what she sent me to school in the following day. The Headmistress was a large, misery guts of a Nun called Sister Borgia, who had a perchance for pain as she hit you with her cane. (Once ALL of Birkenhead's buses had gone on strike, leaving virtually the whole of the school arriving very late. We all had to line up around the outside of the Gym Hall, where Sister Borgia caned every single one of us - My first and only time with a proper cane - for being late.) Many parents (not mine though) complained, but she got away with it, and was universally hated by every pupil in the school. Whilst at St. Winifred's, I did a typing class, where every desk, when lifted, popped up a typewriter. Our teacher Miss Walsh, was a small middle aged Irish Spinster, and some of the girls in the class used to make her cry. They would take bets on who could make her cry first! Because I started at the school in my final year, I was never popular, plus arriving on my first day there with THAT tie and skirt, had, yet again, made me a laughing stock! (One kind teacher had taken me to the Lost Property box and found an aging tie, but a correct one, which she gave me. My Mum was quite put out at first by the gesture, 'We aren't a Charity Case, you know"), but I told her I would get detention if I didn't wear the new one, so she accepted my lie. The skirt, however remained a staple for the rest of my time there. I was never a naughty child, and, although there were barely, if any, books in the house, nor did any of us receive any encouragement with our education, I did quite well at school, particularly in English and cookery. (I'd been cooking a roast dinner and lots of chips since I was nine!) I decided I wanted to become a Lawyer and I had the opportunity to stay on to do my 5th year, and, at first, decided that I would do so. However, my life at that school was made so miserable by the awful Sister Borgia, a large Nun with masses of Rosary Beads around her waist – we could hear her coming from a long way away down the corridors, that half way through the year, I changed my mind and left. With what was going on at home, the abuse, and my new-found sexual exploits, I think I soon realized that school wasn't for me. I didn't enjoy it and I think now that I was just ready to 'grow-up', start work and leave

CRY

home, essentially to get me out of the house, as advancing age did not curb my parents abuse. My Dad continued undressing and masturbating in front of me, but around the time I was 14, my body was developing, and one day, when my brothers were out, and the 3 younger girls were in bed, Dad cupped his hand around my blossoming breast. "Think it's about time you started wearing a bra. You don't wanna get saggy tits!" I remember it as clearly as if it was yesterday. The following day, he must have said something to my Mum, because when I got home from school, there was a bra laying on the table. Not covered, not in a bag, just lying on the table. Being so young, and as the oldest, I had no sisters who had already gone through this, I was mortified, as I had arrived home at the same time as my 2 brothers. The bra itself would have been the cheapest one my Mum could find. (If she could have found me a second-hand one, she would have done!) It was white (as was the usual color then) and it was conical shaped, with white stitching going around and around, ending in a point. To my horror, Mum insisted that I try it on there and then, in front of my brothers and sisters. But I refused. Was Mum happy with that? Of course she wasn't. She was a woman who had always got her own way with her kids. She moved towards me and tried to take off my school blouse – now this is where it just doesn't make sense! All my life she had not once ever acted like a mother, a mother of any kind, and something of a fight ensued, with me pulling away from her and she becoming more and more determined that I should put the wretched bra on, in full view of everyone (My Dad was, thankfully, still at work). I sustained a fair few scratches and some hair pulling, along with a knee to the chin, but there was no way that bra was getting put on in full view of everyone. It was the very first time I had ever acted against her, or attempted to put up any sort of a fight with her. That was when it happened. She turned around and walked into our tiny kitchen and broke down into tears. Now, I had NEVER seen Mum in tears before, neither had my brothers and sisters, and one of my brothers turned on me, accusing of "making Mum cry". Not knowing what to do, I went into the kitchen and asked her if I could go upstairs and put it on (I felt as though she might have suddenly, through a kind of Divine Inspiration, realized that there were certain things a 'mother' was supposed to do to make their children happy, but no, I think she was probably overwhelmed and shocked that I had finally stood-up to her!) I kind of felt sorry for her then, but only for a few moments. "I'm your mother. You shouldn't be fighting with me!" And there, we have 'The Turning Point'. Even though for the next few years until I got married, she would still dig her nails into my arms, or occasionally (though far less than she had been doing since I was very young) pulling me down by my hair and kneeing me in the chin, mouth or face. But I would often try and resist her, or at least make the attacks not so prolonged or as vicious. I was growing up. I recently had an interesting thought. To keep my Dad away from her, is it just possible that Mum knew all along what Dad was doing to me?

CRY

Saying nothing and not intervening? She had had a real 'resentment' against me from a very early age as grandma had singled me out as her favorite grandchild, and allowing my Dad to do what he did to me, and possibly my sisters a few years later. (I will never know as two them have not a single childhood memory) It's just a thought, but one that makes a lot of sense.

TRISH OLLMAN

REBELLION

Life in Cardigan Street went on for the 8 of us in the little terrace house with its concrete back yard and outside toilet. One of my jobs was to get yesterday's newspaper, The Daily Mirror, (my Dad managed to afford to buy a copy every day, along with my parent's 'Ciggies' – but no decent shoes or clothes, sweets, books or games etc. for us kids!) and tear it into neat squares which I then put on a nail in the wall in the outside toilet. (In winter sometimes, it was so cold that the toilet cistern froze and we couldn't flush for days!). One day, I had just got my period and I had no Tampax, so went to look for a sock to use. (I still wonder to this day why my Mum was just SO uncaring, not only to me, but to my other 3 sisters, who probably all went through the same thing, although I don't know, as we don't, and never have had, a relationship where we could talk about these things, plus they have no childhood memories). All children need nurturing, but young teenage girls, well, they need a special type of nurturing in matters of maturing, menstruating, and sex education. But unfortunately for us, we never did get any!) So on this particular day, as I started to go upstairs to find a sock, my Dad, who had been sitting reading his newspaper, shouted, with my brothers and sisters present, "If you're bleeding, use a couple of pieces of that newspaper in the toilet. Don't be using bloody socks!" How the hell did he know? And why humiliate me in front of not only himself (as I was mortified that he had said it), but also in front of the rest of the family? To a young 14-year old girl, in 1966, talking about your periods and anything to do with bodily functions was just the worse sort of humiliation. Again, I can only ask WHY did he do it? Was it some kind of vindictive pleasure he got from it? Did it stem from the sexual abuse? Did he have little or no respect for me? I just don't know.

There are some things that are just too hard to write about when you've lived the life that I have, particularly as of writing, ALL of my 5 siblings are still alive. But one incident I just can't escape mentioning, and I shall just have to accept there may be consequences. One day, I was either 14 or 15, Mum and Dad had gone out. Yes, a rare event. That's probably why what happened did happen. I was laying on my bed (I had moved into the box room by now) when my brother came in and took his clothes off. He persuaded me to take mine off too. Why did I do it? Why? In hindsight, I suppose I was just so use to being 'used' by men (or boys in my brother's case) and he started to try and have sex with me. Unfortunately, I have no explanation as to why I didn't scream or push him away, but suddenly Mum and Dad came back and we hastily got dressed and my brother left. Another time, I had arranged to meet a man (no idea where I met him) but he had a car, and as we were parked at the top of Grange Road (Birkenhead's main shopping area) we were 'making out', or rather HE was making out, I just accepted whatever a man/boy wanted to do to me, when there was a loud knock on the car window. It was my Dad. He must have followed me and been watching all the time, as I had been in the car for quite a while. Naturally, he was furious, and I was frog-marched home and received the leather end of the belt, and sent to bed, my Dad's words of abuse echoing in my head. Later that night, when he came up himself, my Dad came closer along the landing, towards the box room (I still wasn't allowed to have my door shut) and he stood almost in my doorway, undressed, never taking his eyes off me, 'played' with himself until his penis was erect (it seemed to take forever. I think he may have been really annoyed!) and then masturbated. All of this, and for every time, you must understand, that he never, ever, said a single word. But on this particular night I could see the fury in his eyes. Did my Mum know that this was going on? Did she shut it out of her mind? I really don't know. As she always slept on the couch downstairs, she wouldn't have known what went on upstairs. I'm pretty sure my other siblings, especially my brothers, didn't know either, as we were quite close and they would have spoken up about it.

By now, I was completely fed-up living at home. The abuse came from both sides, Dad and his sexual abuse, and Mum with her physical and emotional abuse and neglect. One day, I decided to go, alone, to the cinema, just to escape the realities of my life.

CRY

While I was sitting watching the film, a young man, maybe 19 or 20, came and sat beside me, even though the cinema was mostly empty. He didn't even introduce himself, but put his arm around me. When the film finished, he introduced himself as 'Scott' and asked me if I would like to 'go for a drink' with him. Now, I can only surmise that I looked older than my 15 years, so that's what I did. After the movie had finished, I walked to a Pub with 'Scott' and drank 2 Vodka and Limes. I wonder if you can by this stage guess what happened next? Yep, down the alley we went, and again with me like a block of wood. 'Scott' asked me the question: "Why didn't you come"? Still having no idea what he was talking about, but feeling as though I should maybe 'come', I told him that I had. He then offered to walk me home, which I thought him very gentlemanly to do so, however, when we got to the end of Cardigan Street, there was a Police Car outside my house. It was quite late, so I knew the Police were there for me, as I had been out for quite a long time, so I turned and re-traced my steps away from Cardigan Street. 'Scott' asked me what the matter was and I told him. He walked with me until we reached a railway siding, near Cammell Lairds Shipbuilders. I can't remember what was said, but 'Scott' stayed with me all night in an empty railway carriage. Naturally we had sex again. Did I 'come'? Of course not. The following morning, we left the carriage and walked towards the center of Birkenhead. There was an early morning Café open and 'Scott' bought me a bacon butty (sandwich) and a mug of tea. After we had finished, 'Scott" said goodbye, not offering to meet again, and walked away. I spent most of the rest of the day sitting in St Wherberg's Church or just walking around Birkenhead town center. It would have been about 4pm, with me crossing a road by the church, that my Dad drove past me in his little mini-van. He spotted me and pulled over. I ran like the clappers and down a back alleyway. Soon I heard "Pat, Pat, stop please, come home". And that's what happened. I turned and walked with Dad to his car, and the only thing he said to me all the way home was "You'd better cover that love bite up before your mother sees it". (Thanks 'Scott'!!) Now, again in hindsight, there appears to be a pattern to all this sexual abuse (because that is what it was: I was under 15, right?) Every one of my sexual partners were strangers to me, boys or young men who had just 'picked me up' and then had sex with me. Now, I ask myself what it was about me? I was told by everyone back then that I was 'pretty', so maybe that was it, as I really did love it when anyone said that to me? (We didn't get any kind of praise or kind comments like that at home!) Or maybe I gave them the impression that I was 'Up for it"? (although I think this highly unlikely, given that I hated sex and was most definitely NOT up for it!) Or I was just 'available' and in the wrong place at the wrong time. I think that is the mostly likely explanation! Whatever the reason, the fact remains that through all of these sexual exploits, I felt absolutely nothing and the boy/man I was with at the time really couldn't have cared less!

CRY

I was now 15, and about to leave school. I had decided not to stay on and do a Fifth Year, but to leave in July, the end of the British school year. The year before, Mum and Dad had somehow managed to buy a large tent and a camping stove, and other camping gear, from the Catalogue. (You paid it off at so much every week) That year, we had gone down to Devon and Somerset, my first time away from Merseyside. I remember the smell of the grass in the early morning and the previously unheard mooing of nearby cows. We'd picked unripe cider apples from the trees in the camping ground and tried to eat them. I don't remember anything else from that holiday other than been apprehensive about sleeping in such close quarters with my Dad. However, in 1967, my parents somehow managed another camping holiday. No idea where they'd got the money from as my Mum wasn't working and my dad was only on a Clerk's wage. We piled blankets and pillows into the car (My Dad had purchased it the year before for our holiday in Devon). I can't remember its make or model, but it was small and black. We had a roof rack, so the tent and other things were tied onto that. Now, for children that had never been further than Liverpool across the River Mersey twice, (and once to Devon the previous year), where do you think we might have gone? Yes, of course! We went to France, Belgium and Switzerland. 'THE WALSHES EUROPEAN VACATION' Being summer, the weather was fine, and Mum had a large map on her lap. As we drove off the ferry from Dover, and into Calais in France, my Dad drove on the wrong side of the road, almost immediately we had driven off the boat. This drew the attention of the Police who came to Dad at the driver's window and asked him for his License. We all laughed, as my Dad (who had a stutter) said "Bon Jour Mon Sure". Soon we were on our way to find our first campsite. I remember nothing of this time, only of me and David being sent to buy milk, bread and butter from a shop in Calais, and finding it hard as neither of us spoke a word of French. The only other memory I have is of all the shops in Switzerland lit up in the evening with displays of Watches in their windows. I had tooth ache (I believe there were people, usually men, called 'Dentists', but I'd never met one myself!) and Mum got her ever-present bottle of TCP (a type of antiseptic mouthwash) out and made me put some on the offending tooth. The holiday itself was, for me, a nightmare and I hated every moment of it. We were one blow-up mattress short. Guess who had to have the hard floor? I was almost 15, moody, hormonal, and a teenager who had been abused, both sexually and emotionally, all her life. What was there about a 'Family Holiday' to like? The night before we were due to get the Ferry back from Ostend (in Belgium) to England, Mum and Dad (it was now quite dark) decided to pitch the tent nearby to the Ferry entrance. We were woken the following morning by two burly Belgian policemen, knocking on our tent. It seems we had set up camp right next to the middle of the path that walkers, joggers and bike riders

CRY

used. We were easily able to understand the word 'MOVE', even if it was in French.

Once we were back on English soil, our journey home to Birkenhead, for some reason, took us through London. (No myriad of Motorways then). We stopped off at my Aunty and Uncle's house for a visit. (it was my Dad's niece and her family.) It was while we were there that my parents and Aunty & Uncle went out to the Pub, leaving us 6 children alone, along with their own 3. At some point, later that night, my Uncle came home alone. Why, I don't know, but as I sat on the couch, he came and sat beside me, pushed me back and started to 'explore' my young body. I can remember his hand squeezing my breasts, then his fingers going down below. He pulled out his penis and tried to grab my hand and make me get hold of it, but luckily, the rest of the Adults came in just at that moment, and my Uncle hastily zipped up his flies. I can remember feeling dirty and used, but, WHY?? Why didn't I shout it from the rooftops? Again, I can only think that at that age, I had been suffering from sexual abuse for years, and maybe it was a man's 'right' to do these things to girls? After we left the following day, we made our way through London to the main road back to Birkenhead. In the back of the small car, sat all of us six children, all squashed together (No seat belts in those days!). Close to the center of the City, David said "Mum, Pat (me) won't move over" (Don't forget there were eight of us, all squashed into the back seat of a tiny car!). With that my Mum did what she always did, she leant over to the back of the car and dug her nails into my arm, making me cry out. What happened next, I can remember as though it were just yesterday. For reasons unknown, (maybe he actually DID feel something for me?) Dad pulled the car over and stopped. He said to Mum "Why can't you just leave her alone?" Now, I find this to be amazing, as he had NEVER stuck up for any of us kids before, and especially so for me, due to his own abuse. Mum took this 'telling off' by Dad badly, and stormed out of the car. Peter, always a 'Mummy's boy', also got out and followed Mum. My Dad turned to me and said "You'd better go after her as well". What happened next makes no sense to me whatsoever, even all these years later. I got out of the car, but walked in the opposite direction to the way Mum and Peter had gone. My Dad, sitting in the car, made no attempt to stop me, and I wish I'd have had the chance to ask him why, before he died. I continued walking until I was well out of sight of the car. I looked in my old bag that I was carrying, and saw that it contained only a lipstick (I could never wear it, as Mum didn't allow make-up, plus I had stolen it from a Chemist by my Auntie's house the day before) and a red pen, plus the ticket from the boat from Calais to Dover, which I had kept as a souvenir. I had not a single penny. Not knowing what to do, or where I was going, I finally arrived at a bus stop. When a bus arrived, it said 'Battersea' on the front, so I got on, then gave the Conductor a false name and address, telling him I had lost my purse (You could do that back then, where

CRY

they would expect you to send them the money when you arrived home.) I got off the bus when it reached Battersea High Street and walked aimlessly (I still had no idea what I was going to do. I just knew that I was 'running away' and this caused me some anxiety.) Suddenly, I was in front of a Tobacconist shop, and in the window, was a card, advertising for a 'Nanny" to three children. It gave an address in Battersea but no phone number (Privately owned phones were a rarity then). Looking around me, I found an empty cigarette box on the floor and wrote the address with my lipstick, on it. I went inside the Tobacconist and asked directions then set off. Patmore Gardens, when I reached it, was a large block of flats, and I soon found the flat number. Knocking on the door, I got no answer, so, with no other option, I sat on the stairs and waited. My memory won't allow me to remember how long I waited, but eventually, a man in his mid-thirties, Tony, came home and when I told him I'd come about the job, he invited me in. I told him that I was 19 and that all of my luggage had been stolen when I arrived at Kings Cross Railway Station (to account for my not having a single thing!) and he seemed to believe me. Eventually, his three children came home. They were aged 8, 10 and 12. Two girls and a boy. I remember little else, apart from being terrified every time I heard a car outside (I was convinced it was the Police coming to get me!). That evening, Tony took me to his local pub, to show me off, I suppose it was thought that I was his 'new' girlfriend. I drank Vodka and Lime and he bought us a bag of chips on the short walk home. I remember being terrified that the Police had tracked me down. I just knew that I didn't want to go home. After using the bathroom, and then Tony doing the same, we just got into his bed. He never asked my permission, he just went ahead, and with very little foreplay (not that it mattered to ME!) had sex with me. I was not quite 15. He was 37 and must have thought all of his Christmases had come at once!

I lived with Tony for four months. He would give me money, usually ten shillings, every day, and I would buy food and necessities for myself. Scott, his son, was only a few years younger than me, and we got on really well. But still there was always the anxiety in the back of my mind that the Police would arrive at any minute to take me back home, and I sure as hell didn't want that to happen. It was during this time that I, for some unknown reason, (surely fate couldn't have been that cruel?) wrote to a boy I had recently met when I went with a gang of girlfriends, to the Birkenhead Boyd Club. I had 'done the rounds' going out with the small group of boys, as had the other girls, until only one remained. He had never said a single word during the whole time we had been going there, quite a few months, and was very pale, with dark curly, almost afro-style hair. His name, I found out was (we'll call him) 'Mike'. Mike's parents ran a Pub back in Birkenhead. Even though I barely knew him, and even though I knew he was not like your average teenage boy, I now wonder why on earth I was to write to him, a boy I barely knew or liked, and put "I still love you".

CRY

To my amazement, he wrote back and said "I still love you too". It was like a red rag to a bull, somebody telling ME they loved me! I have no idea why, but Tony paid for my bus fare to go back up to Birkenhead. I went straight to Mike's parent's Pub and spent the evening upstairs (his Mum and Dad were downstairs all evening) with Mike and I listening to his records, Procol Harum, The Spencer Davies Group, The Small Faces, and The Beatles Sergeant Peppers album, amongst others. During the evening, even though he knew I was a run-a-way, living in London, he barely said two words to me, and made no attempt whatsoever of putting his arm around me, or kissing me in any fashion, the way every other man or boy had done for the last few years. I thought him very odd, but, with nowhere else to go, and the novelty of living with Tony wearing off, I suppose I just went along with it. When it came time for me to leave, he never even asked me where I was staying that night. He just muttered 'night' and went back indoors. After that, I left the Pub and had to find somewhere to sleep. I made my way over to St Wherberg's Church graveyard and laid on the floor, my coat over me, but a few moments later, I heard a scurrying noise close by. It was a homeless tramp, also set on sleeping there. I jumped up and walked down Conway Street. Now, these days, at my age, I would say that any teenager getting into a stranger's car was a bit stupid. But no. Not me back then. A car pulled up alongside of me (I was less than 5 minutes from home but still a run-a-way!) and the guy asked me if I wanted a lift, to where, he never asked. But in I got nonetheless. As we drove passed our Chippie (Chip Shop) he asked if I had eaten. When I said no, he told me to stay in the car, and he went over and bought fish and chips. As I was eating them, I hadn't noticed but he had driven to Moreton Shore, a hive of activity during the days in summer, but cold and pitch black at this time of the year and at around 11pm. Three guesses what happened next?? Anyone?? Yep, he was only after one thing, but hey, I was grateful, as I got fish and chips out of it, and the back of the car was at least warm! Afterwards, he asked me where I wanted to go, and the only place I could think of was Liverpool's Lime Street Railway Station.

So, there I am sitting on a bench inside Lime Street Station at 2am. Not another single person there. Just me, aged just 15. All of a sudden, a Policemen appeared. Now bear in mind I'm a run-a-way, and he asks me what I'm doing there. Quick as a flash, I tell him I'm waiting for the 6.30am train to London. And he believes me. Doesn't ask my name, nothing. So much for the Merseyside Police Force. Bored, I wandered up and out of the Station and came to the Ribble Bus Station, which runs alongside Lime Street Station. There was a line of red Ribble Busses, and one of them was being cleaned. The cleaner told me I could sleep across one of the benches if I wanted to. As I was getting comfortable, I wonder if you can guess what the cleaner did? Yes, I'm sure you're right yet again. He got on top of me and 20 seconds later he

CRY

was doing his flies up and went back to work. Once again, I took it as a reward for the guy letting me sleep on the bus. It was how you rewarded someone being nice to you. Wasn't it? I got off the bus as I didn't want it to happen again, and went back to my lonely bench in Lime Street Station. I sat there until 6am then hitch-hiked back though the Mersey Tunnel to discreetly watch Mike and his parents go on their annual holiday to his Auntie's in Exeter, Devon. I stood hidden behind a post in the block of flats opposite, and watched as they piled into the car, wishing I was going too, although to this day, I wonder why? Probably the excitement of going to Devon, which had always been my favorite place in the UK. Instead, once Mike and his parents had driven off, I made my way to the motorway, via New Chester Road, and hitch-hiked back down to London. I was lucky, as this was around the time of Fred and Rose West and their multiple murders of unsuspecting and vulnerable hitchhikers. Sound like me? It sure does. I consider myself very lucky indeed, as I would have fit their horrific, evil, stereotype right down to the ground. Once on the Motorway, my thumb stuck out in the hitch hiking pose, a truck stopped for me and the driver took me as far as he was going. I got out and stuck my thumb out again, and almost immediately another truck stopped. I got in, barely able to keep my eyes open, as I'd been awake all of the previous night in Lime Street Station. After a while, we stopped at a Motorway Services. The driver bought me a cup of tea and a sandwich, and while we ate, he tried to put his hand up my skirt. I hit his hand off so hard that my tea went all over him. To his credit, he did apologize and took me all the way to Tony's flat in London. He even gave me him and his wife's and his name and address on a piece of paper, and told me to call if I ever was in any trouble. It was around midnight when he dropped me off and I used my key to Tony's flat. Once inside, I heard noises coming from the living room. I crept up and there was Tony sitting next to a blonde, middle-aged woman, his arm around her, and they were both kissing and cuddling. Suddenly, I no longer wanted to be there, but it was late and I had nowhere else to go, so I went and got into bed with Ton's young daughter, and early the next morning, crept out of the flat, leaving my key on the hall table. I never heard from him again.

With nowhere to go, and no money, I headed for Kings Cross Station, again giving the bus conductor a false name and address. Looking on the benches, I found a discarded copy of last night's newspaper. In the Situations Vacant section, I saw an advert for a Nanny in Golders Green, a North London suburb. I rang the number, reverse charge, telling the woman who answered the same story of stolen bags that I had told Tony. She told me to get in a taxi and gave me the address, and that once I'd arrived, she would come out and pay for it. I found out that the couple were Jewish, (Let's call them 'Elisa and Adam'), and they had 2 small daughters aged 1 and 3. They both worked during the day and I had to take care of the children. The girls were only about one and two, but I had plenty

CRY

of experience raising children, with my own siblings, so was quite confident. For the first time, I lived in close quarters with a man who made no attempt at acting indecently with me. They were a lovely couple and the little girls well behaved. But soon, as is usual in these situations, my duties became more and more. I no longer just had to look after the girls but I was also expected to clean the whole 3-bedroom house. Deciding that I wanted to go back up to Birkenhead and see Mike, (In hindsight, I now wish I now knew WHY?? Maybe I'd been struck with sudden onset Mental Illness?) I put the 2 girls down for their lunchtime sleep, then packed my things and just walked out. It is to my shame that I left those 2 babies alone in the house. I hitch-hiked again up the M1 and was soon back in Birkenhead. (A few weeks later, I had the cheek to ring their mother to see if they were alright, and boy, did I get a (well-deserved) blasting from her. She said that, luckily, she had rung me at lunchtime, and when she'd got no answer, she had rushed home. It haunts me to this day!)

In retrospect, I now wonder why on earth I would have wanted to go back to see Mike. Maybe it was because he never, ever tried to even kiss me, never mind do anything else, as all the other boys and men in my life had done. He had absolutely no conversation or empathy, or emotions and wasn't even attractive. But go back I did. I was 15 and knew nothing of the way of the world, nor of emotional abuse, but more of that later. I once again had nowhere to go, but I still had a small amount of money left from what Tony had given me (I didn't get paid at the Jewish couple's house, just my board). So I got on a National Express bus that took me back up to Liverpool. Mike was his usual self, not saying barely a word, with no kissing or touching (which suited, but confused me at the same time) and we sat and drank Coke and listened to his records. When it came time for me to leave, he never asked where I was going, he just said goodbye. So where was I to go? Last time I had visited Birkenhead, I had been picked up by a stranger in a car, then spent the night at Lime Street Station, and used twice in one night, as a sex toy for some dirty old man, so I wasn't going to make that mistake again, was I? Sorry to disappoint, but, while I wasn't picked up by a man in a car, I was 'picked up' while I was in the Chip Shop getting a bag of chips. His name was Terry, and he lived in a room in a large house on Whetstone Lane. Now, having nowhere to go that night, even though it doesn't excuse what I did, what followed does show how desperate I was. I was 15, a run-a-way back in Birkenhead (not 10 minutes from home) and had nowhere to sleep. So yes, I went home with Terry. He had to sneak me into his room, as girls in rooms weren't allowed by his Landlady. We'd been in bed about half an hour, when the Landlady stormed into the room, screaming at me to 'get out' and telling Terry that tomorrow he could pack his bags and leave. So, I just got dressed and left. Just walked down the stairs and out into the cold night. Terry never offered to meet up again. He just said "sorry". And that was it. I never

CRY

saw him again. There was a 'bombie' (a site of nothing but dirt, that he been bombed during the War) nearby, and someone had dumped an old car there, so that's where I spent the night, freezing cold and crying. Being a run-a-way is not much fun, especially when you're trying to get a bit of sleep in an abandoned old car. I saw Mike the following day for about an hour, he never asked where I'd spent the night, despite knowing I was a run-a-way, then I made my way over to Liverpool to catch the 9am bus back down to London.

Once again, having nowhere to go (I'd left the Jewish family.) so I got off the bus at Charring Cross Station and again went inside the large Railway Station to see if I could find a copy of the day's newspaper. Again, I was lucky. In the Situations Vacant section, an Indian man who owned a café (Can't remember where in London) wanted someone to help out as a waitress. I still had a little money, so I rang him. He told me the address, and I got the Tube to the address he'd given me. I can't even remember his name, but I do remember that I had a very close call with drugs while I was there. Even though recreational drugs had been used by the rich and famous for many years, street drugs in 1966-67 where only starting to become popular. One day I took an order from a table of six young people. After they had given me their order, one of them, a young guy, asked me if I'd like to go to a party that night. Naturally I said yes. He then produced a small pack of pills from his pocket and told me that 'one of these will make you feel as though you're floating'. Well that sounded good to me. The guy asked me for ten shillings, (10 bob (slang for shillings), quite a lot of money back then) which I willingly handed over, and he wrote down an address on a scrap of paper, where he said the party would be, and where I would get my ten bob tablet! After work that night, I made a real effort with my appearance, bought a cheap lipstick and washed my hair. The Indian man asked me what time I would be back and I remember saying "Probably not till morning!" (I was a 'grown-up' now, wasn't I?). The next thing I remember after a long Tube journey, followed by an even longer walk, was that upon arrival at the 'Party House (Where I was to get my SPEED tablet) was nothing more than a vacant block of land. I was mortified, not so much as there was no party and no speed tablet, but that I had wasted 10 bob, probably almost half a week's wage for me. I now look back and think how lucky I was that it happened as it did. If I had become hooked on Speed, Marijuana, then Heroin possibly, may have followed, and a life of drugs for a girl who had so little self-confidence and was starting to feel so 'used' sexually, would have been a very easy route for me to take. I count this to be one of the luckiest escapes of my life, even if I did lose ten bob! Life could have turned out very different for me if I'd have had that first Speed tablet.

I lived (in every sense of the word) with the Indian guy for only about 2 months. One day, I came home

CRY

from the shops to find him in quite a state. Someone from Social Security (When I started work there, I had stupidly given him my last place legitimate place of work, T.J. Hughes in Birkenhead, (I was a run-a-way! Why on earth would I have given him my last official place of work?) had been around telling him I was wanted back in Birkenhead by the Police. The Indian man panicked and told me to go up and pack my things and leave. I stole four packs of cigarettes (I had tried to smoke but hated it, so have no idea why I took those four packets.) I had been gone from home for 5 months. I had cut and dyed my hair and I was wearing fishnet stockings (tights weren't to become popular for another year or so.) So, I looked nothing like the Pat Walsh who had ran away from her parents and siblings from the car, in London back in the summer. What to do now? I think that maybe I had had enough of being on the run, sick of all the men I worked for (apart from the Jewish man) thinking they could just have me in their bed, have sex with me, and just basically use me. So, I used what little money I had left and got on a bus back to Liverpool. It was about 8pm when I arrived at the Pub and Mike, the only place I could go. He said he was 'going down to get some 'ciggies' (Being a Pub, there were always cigarettes stored under the stairs, and Mike had been smoking since he was 12) and I thought nothing of this. But hang on, where was he? He'd been gone for ages. All of a sudden I heard loud footsteps coming up the stairs. A second later, the doorway was filled with a giant Policeman. "Pat Walsh? You've led us a merry dance, haven't you? We've been looking for you for a very long time. Come on. Down with me!" And that was it. The end of my days as a run-a-way, and the start of a whole new chapter in my life.

WHEN YOUNG IS TOO YOUNG

The big Policeman led me downstairs where a timid-looking Mike was standing in the doorway, his head down. Beside him was, horror of horrors, my Mum, a ciggie in her mouth, face looking downwards. Outside, I was greeted with not one, but THREE Police cars (what on earth did they think they were dealing with? A gun-toting Bonnie and Clyde?) and their corresponding Officers. All the drinkers in the Pub had also come out

CRY

to see what the commotion was about. To say I was mortified with embarrassment is an understatement. I found out later that my Mum had been around to Mike's Mum after I had run away in London, and told her to get Mike to tell her if I came to Birkenhead to visit him. The first few times I had visited, Mike had said nothing, but this time, him 'going down to get a pack of ciggies' was really him running around to Cardigan Street, about a 5-minute walk from the Pub, to tell my Mum I was there, hence the police. They took me and Mum in the back of a Police Car to the police Station at Woodside and quizzed me on where I'd been. I invented a wife for Tony and said I'd been the Nanny, and left it at that. Once back home, I did something really, really stupid. I took out two cigarettes from one of the boxes I had taken from the Indian Café in London, lit one for myself (even though I didn't smoke??) and offered my Mum one! She managed to keep her cool, something that must have been hard for her, and told me to "get rid of them before your father sees them" (he was out when I'd arrived back home and I had to sit for a good hour in trepidation, awaiting his return!) When he did arrive home, my Dad took me into the 'unused' front room and told me he thought I was now a 'bad influence' on the other kids in the house and he wanted me gone by tomorrow morning. There was I, 15, with purple hair (very 'hippy' back then, and fishnet stockings. I must have looked like a Hooker! (Hey, maybe that's why I attracted so much male attention?) A little later, just before I went up to bed, Mum said "Do you want to leave?" Having nowhere else to go, I told her no, I wanted to stay. "I'll have a word with your Dad. You'll be Ok"!! The very first time in my entire 15 years, she had said something nice to me. I walked on air for days. I've no idea what she said to him, but the subject was never mentioned again and life went on as though I'd never been away.

After 'dobbing me in' I didn't speak to Mike for a few weeks, then, one day, I was walking home from Grange Road, Birkenhead's main shopping street, when he was walking towards me. I can't really remember, but I think I invited myself over to the Pub to 'play our records'. And so began the next stage of our lives. I'm sorry to keep asking you, but WHY? Why didn't I run a mile? I've mentioned all of his non-attributes, and I was quite an attractive girl (no, I'm not boasting, but I had been told by many people that I was, so it's just a fact.) so I wonder to this very day why I set the entire rest of my life on what was to be a very unhappy course. So, Mike and I started to go upstairs at the Pub and play records. In those days, it was easy to get a job, and I got one as an Office Junior at E. R. Squibbs, a large Pharmaceutical Manufacturing Company in Moreton. Opposite was the Cadbury Factory and at first I loved the smell as I walked into work, but after a week or two, Yuk! It made us all feel sick! (I have written of my exploits at Squibbs - as 'Hettie' the Office Junior – in my Book, 'The Office Girls') Life at work was so different to life as a schoolgirl. I was still treated as 'the Junior' by the

CRY

other girls in the office, but I loved being around adults. The other good thing, for me, was that I was only around women all day. However, that didn't stop me from once again being used by a man. This time it was one who was on the same bus as I went home. We will call him 'Pete'. One day, 'Pete' came and sat beside me on the bus. He told me how pretty I was (You can guess what's coming by now!) and was soon holding my hand. He suggested we get off the bus at Birkenhead Park, and like a lamb to the slaughter, I did as I was told. I wish I knew why I never put up any resistance. It was the words, telling me how pretty I was, how lovely my eyes were etc. etc. that was what I so badly craved, that and the attention. Also, take into account the fact that boys and men had been using me since I was 13, (Not to mention my Dad's attentions!) meant that you just did what you were told. As my parents were extremely strict and abusive, I was brought up to do as I was told. That's the only explanation I can think of. 'Pete" was the second man who asked me why I didn't 'Come'. This was still a mystery to me and I never had the courage to ask what it meant. I remember walking home from Birkenhead Park on that day feeling dirty and like a block of wood.

I stayed at Squibbs for only about 6 months. Making tea and photocopying all day just didn't do it for me. I wanted to be a lawyer, standing in a Courtroom fighting for the Prosecution (I was reading Agatha Christie's 'Witness for the Prosecution' at the time) but not having the necessary qualifications to go to University to study Law, I got a job as a Typist (I couldn't Type) at British Rail's Head Office, in Liverpool. Every day, I would go over on the train from Hamilton Square, down in the lift to the platform, and then walk to British Rail's Headquarters. On my first day, I was sat at a small desk, along with rows of a couple of dozen other typists. My desk had an electric typewriter on it, and the Supervisor gave me a hand-written letter from one of the bosses to type. Being me, I couldn't turn the dam thing on. I had no idea how to. Luckily, there was a kind girl behind me and she told me to just plug it into the socket on the floor. The beast sprang to life and I started to try and type the letter. I had been good at English at school, and knew how a letter should be laid out etc. but my failing was that I just couldn't get the hand of touch typing. Like at Squibbs, there was a Supervisor sitting facing us at the top of the room, and as she was easily able to see me (My desk was very close to the front) she soon realized that I was making many, many mistakes, and had to keep starting again. (I think screwing up my copy paper into a ball and continuously throwing it into the waste paper bin every time I made a mistake, may have given away the fact that I really wasn't a typist!) And so it came as no surprise to me when, I shortly after found myself sitting at another desk, this time in the Drawing Office. My job was to answer the phone for the Architects and Clerks who worked there. While at Squibbs, I had been going over to Liverpool as often as I could, to the Silver Blades Ice Rink in Prescott

CRY

Road. Sometimes I would have no money (my Mum took almost all of my wages, leaving me only with my bus fare – Yes, nothing much had changed at home) so would hitch-hike through the Mersey Tunnel and do the half hour walk to the Ice Rink. I went there so often that the doorman got to know me (He wore an old Soldier's Uniform and had 2 fingers missing off his hand) and I would just walk in without paying. (As 'Hettie' in my book, 'The Office Girls', I'm afraid to say I was a very naughty girl whilst at that Ice Rink!) After skating, and if I had the money, I would go across to the Café across the road and have egg and chips (You need to read 'The Office Girls' if you are wondering where I got the money from for this treat!). Meanwhile, back at British Rail, I would, during my lunch hour, hurry back on the train to Birkenhead, and meet Mike, who I still seeing, (He had stayed on at School to do his fifth year) and we would walk around Hamilton Square holding hands (well, rather me holding his hand!) It was during this time that I started to get morning sickness, but what on earth could be causing it?

It's surprising that in 1968, we knew so little about pregnancy and all the associated things that went with it. But I was only 15, Mike, slightly older at just 16. In April, a year after we had met, Mike had gone to Spain for a week with his school. I missed him so much (WHY?) that one day I went into the Pub and told his Mum, who was a real dragon, that I had left a book up in Mike's room. I just wanted to go up and be near his things. I remember picking up one of his jumpers and crying into it. We had been 'going out' for a year (although this had been broken up by my time in London) and Mike had only just started to kiss me (Actually it was ME who had started kissing him!). Looking back, he was exactly what I needed at the time: a boy who didn't want to have sex with me, but there was no other attraction whatsoever. And me? I was devoid of any emotion whatsoever, and was unable to know or feel what love was like. During my time at British Rail in Liverpool 1968, I would rush back on the train to Birkenhead to meet up with Mike for my lunch break. We would just walk through Hamilton Square, talking and telling of that day's events (Well, it was me who did all the talking), and then every Friday night we would go to the Capitol Chinese Restaurant by Hamilton Square, and have the same thing every week; curry king prawns and rice! We did this for about six months. When Mike had come home from Spain, I don't know whether I wanted him or not, or, as I had thought until recently, was I just curious as to WHY Mike didn't want me. Even though I had absolutely no sexual urges or desires, when Mike came home, we were upstairs in the Pub, his parent's downstairs, and I, out of sheer frustration with his lack of any kind of intimacy, 'helped' Mike to have sex with me. It was his first time, and he had had no inclination during the year we'd been going out, to do anything with me. We didn't do it again for quite a while, however, that first time was now the cause of my morning sickness. I had gone to the family Doctor telling him I felt sick every

CRY

day (how naïve was I??) and after telling me to pee into a specimen jar, he floored me with the news that I was pregnant. All those times with those other boys and men, all generally one-night-stands, and the four months living with Tony in London, and they never once used protection. And yet here Mike and I are, doing it for the first time, again without protection, and I'd become pregnant. I filled in some forms at the Doctors and walked home absolutely delighted. A child of my own. Someone who I could love unconditionally. Naturally, I couldn't tell my parents (My Dad was still sexually abusing me, and as he never actually 'did' the sex act with me, only on himself with me, an unwilling participant, I knew it could only be Mike's baby, as I hadn't had sex with anyone else for a long time) I told Mike in the Pub's kitchen. He never said a word. (More on Mike's lack of speech and any emotional feelings later) I was lying in bed one morning and my Mum came into my room and sat on the edge. She made some small talk, while all the time I was thinking, why on earth is she in here. She never ever came upstairs, never mind into my room. Then came the bombshell. "Why didn't you tell me you were pregnant?" Now, it might have been the Swinging Sixties, but for a 15-year old to become pregnant in 1968 really wasn't acceptable, nor was it the done thing. I'm sure it happened, but not to anyone I knew. "Do you want to keep it?" she asked me. Yes. Mum said that St Catherine's Hospital in Tranmere could give me an abortion, and explained to me what this meant, but I told her no, I wanted to keep it. I wanted what this little embryo would become, a baby of my own. Mum said "Do you want me to go and tell Mike's Mum?", so that what she did. Mike's Mum, however, was having none of it. Her baby boy had been probably raped by this whore. There was no wat her Mike would have willingly gotten me pregnant. His future was already mapped out, she'd told my Mum. He was to be shipped off to his Aunty's in Canada to learn a trade. She offered me fifty pounds, an absolute fortune then, to have an abortion, when I said "No" she offered me eighty pounds to have it, give it to her to bring up (Look at how she 'brought' up Mike? What a great Mum she'd been to him.) and to move away from Merseyside. I said "No" to all her requests. As the months went by, my morning sickness continued. I was due to have the baby around Christmas time and it was now July, coming up to my 16th birthday. I enjoyed wearing a maternity dress, my only one, putting my hands protectively across my growing bump. For the first time in my life I actually felt something. I felt proud. Proud and happy at the little being growing inside me. Shortly after, and especially due to the sickness, (which I'd first felt while I was at the café opposite the Ice Rink) I gave up work, bought a gorgeous, big navy and white Silver Cross pram from a girl I knew who lived near to Mike's Pub, and kept trying to get his Mum to give her permission for us to be married, (Back then, in England, you had to be 18 before you could marry without your parent's consent, but in Scotland, it was only 16). For once in their lives, my parents stepped up to the plate. Dad

CRY

gave us a few pounds and drove us to Hamilton Square Station, and they both knew of our intentions, vowing to not tell Mike's Mum when she would definitely come around looking for him, or trying to get my parents to tell her where he was. And so, on 27th July 1968, Mike and I boarded a big, red Ribble Bus in Liverpool, bound for Scotland. The night before, I had asked Mike to pack a case and we had snuck it round to my house, ready to go the next day. He never once put up any semblance of resistance. New once expressed an opinion on the forthcoming baby, he just went along with it. The journey to Gretna Green, our intended destination (it was a big, well-known place for run-a-ways wanting to be married, as it was on the English/Scottish border) seemed exciting. We had seven pounds between us which we had no idea how far that would take us. I'd bough a one-way ticket to Scotland (again, WHY?) and we, or I really should say, I, never gave a thought to how we would live on seven pounds. After a very long 10-hour bus trip, we decided not to get off at Gretna Green, as there was a large new Police Station opposite the bus stop. As Mike was, to all intents and purposes, a run-a-way, we thought it too risky and the police station really put us off, so we stayed on the bus until the end of the line, Edinburgh. By now it was gone 10pm and we just wanted to sleep. Right opposite the bus stop, was a Bed and Breakfast. As we just had the grand sum of seven pounds, at that point we weren't thinking about money (Nor was Mike thinking about anything else!) we took a room with a double bed, and ate what was left of the sandwiches we'd brought with us. We then got undressed and got into our first bed together. Surely, this was to be the night when Mike would realize what was happening, woo me, and make mad passionate love to me? You're joking, right? This isn't a Barbara Cartland novel. Now, I'm hoping by now that you know I have no sexual desires whatsoever. I'm like a piece of wood and get no enjoyment whatsoever, not even a flutter, out of any sort of sexual acts. But that first night, in a bed together for the very first time, I EXPECTED it. Well, you do, don't you? Mike was a 16-year old boy whose body should have been raging with hormones. I was not unattractive and I had a good body. But what does Mike do? He says goodnight and turns over and goes to sleep. I don't know why, but to this day I get really annoyed when I think of it! I think I feel somehow aggrieved, and at the time, it made my very low self-confidence even lower. Even though I didn't like sex, I still think that Mike should have at least made an effort. Any sort of effort would have done!! At the end of the day, I now realize that I wanted nothing more than to be taken care of, basically I wanted to be loved, cherished and given the attention I so desperately craved. Was Mike to be the person who met my needs? I doubted it!

KILTS & SPORRENS

CRY

Once in Scotland, we found out that we couldn't 'Put up the Banns' until I was actually 16 (which was in two-day's time), and until we had lived in Scotland for four weeks. Four Weeks! We didn't even have enough money for four days, let alone four weeks. It was a Saturday, the day after our arrival in Edinburgh. We had spent three pounds on the Bed and Breakfast the night before, and had four pounds left, and as we walked down the main Street, Princess Street, looking up at the might Edinburgh Castle, high on the hill, and at all the wonderful, previously unseen shops, with people talking in a strange accent, we wondered what we could rent with such little money. We'd decided (or should I say I'd decided, Mike couldn't 'decide' on anything, even if his life depended on it!) that we would say that we had actually been living in Edinburgh for four weeks on the Monday, when we went to put up the Banns at the Registry Office. Walking up Princess Street, we came upon a small shop that just did rentals. Yes, they had a small room in a house, for rent, at two pounds fifty a week, so we happily took it. We took a bus to the District of Morningside, on the outskirts of the City. The house was a large early century terraced property and the room itself turned out to be a small attic bedroom at the top of the house, in the gables. It was a Sunday and we had fifty pence to find something to eat and drink until we could go to the pawn shop the following day.

That night, again, in bed, Mike turned over to go to sleep. Luckily, I was feeling sick (as I did do right until the end of my pregnancy) and as I wasn't interested in sex, I didn't mind. But I did think it odd that a boy of his age should be having as much sex as he could get, but Mike was never interested. So yet again, I felt totally rejected, ugly, and unlovable. (I must say at this point that back then, I wasn't the strong, capable woman that I was to become. I was a naïve 16-year old who didn't know why she did, or allowed others to do, the things she did. It was a very confusing time for me, as I had been 'popular' with boys and men (not to mention my Dad's attentions since I was seven!) since the age of 13, yet here I was with a boy the same age as me who wasn't remotely interested in me the way I thought males of any age should have been.) Anyway, the following morning, a Monday, our first job, as it was my 16th birthday, was to go and put the Banns up at Morningside Registry Office. This was as easy as showing our Birth Certificates and filling in a form, then a Notice with our names on was then put in the window – the idea being, that anyone who saw this, and wanted to object to the marriage, could do so, and they had 7 days in which to do it. It also meant that we had to wait eight days until we could get married. I should add that there was never any discussion, either with Mike or his parents, about the fact that the decent thing to do WAS to get married. Back then, it was just taken for granted that you would if you were pregnant. So back to Edinburgh, with putting up the Banns ticked off the list, our next stop was the Pawn Shop. We didn't have a penny to our name so had no choice but to pawn the few possessions we did have. They were

CRY

Mike's new-fangled hi-tech (he'd got it for Christmas) electric razor. Fortunately, he wasn't that fond of it, as it had made small cuts all over his face. Then there was my second-hand, thin, wedding ring, that I had bought, also at a Pawn Shop, in Birkenhead, for the occasion. And finally, Mike's thick overcoat, which we'd bought with us 'just in case' it was cold. I think in total, we received ten shillings for the lot.

The eight days we had to wait (the Banns had to be in the Registry Office's window for seven days) seemed to drag on forever. By now, I was about five months pregnant and boy did the morning (try 'all day') sickness kick in. We'd gotten on a bus to take us into the center of Edinburgh one day, and I had to jump off at the traffic lights to be sick in the gutter. I ended up going to a local Doctor who gave me anti-sickness tablets. Now this was the era of Thalidomide, but thank God my tablets were not these, however they never worked, and I was to be sick every day until I had Stephen in December. The night before the 'Big Day' and I washed my filthy fawn coat for the wedding the following day's nuptials. (I hadn't noticed it was so dirty, especially around the neck. But when you barely wash, it's bound to happen. There were no showers then, and it was the norm for most families just to get a 'swill' occasionally, and then a once weekly an 'all over wash', which was supposed to be 'all over' but often was just the hands and face) I walked up the street to where I had seen some roses in someone's front garden and picked two. I used my last sixpence to buy a bar of Cadbury's chocolate and used the silver paper off it to put around the rose stems. I got 2 small safety pins off the lady who owned the house and attached them. We now had buttonholes for our big day. However, I speak too soon: we didn't. I had put the roses in a glass of water that night, but by the following morning the petals had all but fallen off. They were unwearable, so no buttonholes. Still I had my nice clean coat. Only problem was it was still wet, but I had no choice but to wear it. Now to spruce Mike up. He did have a shirt and a thin black tie, and I had washed the shirt and it was sort of dry. Remember that electric razor we'd pawned the week before? Well it had cut his face in half a dozen places. So, can someone tell me, please, why I thought it a good idea that I stick Band Aids all over his face? With the buttonholes unwearable due to the petals now falling off, my wet coat, and Mike with Band Aid pieces all over his face, what a sight we must have looked.

At last the wedding party (just Me and Mike) set off for Morningside Registry Office. It wasn't quite nine, so we had to wait outside for a while. Once inside, the Registrar asked us for ten shillings for the Marriage License. Hey? Nobody had told us we had to pay! But the man was really lovely and when he'd heard our story, he told us we could pay him once we were back home. Phew! I breathed a sigh of relief. I've no idea why I felt that we had to be married, but I did, and found the whole thing really stressful. Then the Registrar asked us where our witnesses were. What?

CRY

Again, nobody had told us about needing witnesses. I thought that was it. No marriage for us. But he then said "Go outside and see if you can find 2 people who will be witnesses for you". So that's what we did, and amazingly, as soon as we stepped outside, 2 little old ladies, carrying shopping baskets, were approaching. I must have had a 'look' on my face as I didn't even have to ask. One of them said "Oooo do you want us to be witnesses (the fact that we were both standing outside the Registry Office might have been a bit of a give-away!). And so, with everything in place, the 'happy' bride and her groom were ready for the nuptials to go ahead. One of our little old ladies took off her own wedding ring and lent it to Mike to put on my finger (We'd pawned the one I'd brought, remember?) and after the ceremony had ended, they gave us a pound. I thanked them most sincerely and we were now able to pay the Registrar his ten bob, but after saying goodbye to our two unlikely witnesses, we had to rush back to our Boarding House and collect our bags, then almost at a run, with Mike carrying the two heavy suitcases, we reached the Bus Depot just as our Ribble Bus back to Liverpool was leaving. I waved like a woman possessed at the driver and he stopped and let us on. There was no Conductor on that bus in Edinburgh, but we knew that one would get on to check people's tickets at some point. Now, we didn't have a return ticket back home. We'd only been able to afford to buy a one-way ticket from Liverpool to Edinburgh. So when the Conductor did get on, about half an hour later, he reached us, and I handed him our one-way ticket from Liverpool to Edinburgh. "This is the wrong ticket, luv," he told me. Quick as a whistle, I doubled the price I'd paid for the original one-way ticket in my head and told the Conductor that that was how much we'd paid. "Oh, they must have made a mistake in Liverpool. Don't worry. I'll sort it out." It was as easy as that. As the coach passed through towns and cities on Scotland's east coast, the only thing Mike and I had to eat was a half a box of Ritz Crackers and a jar of Roses Lime Marmalade, the only food we'd had left in Edinburgh. On one of the 'toilet' stops, we were able to buy a cup of tea with the money left over from the pound our witnesses had given to us. Eventually, that night, arriving home in Birkenhead, I was to wonder if married life was going to be one long struggle as today had been. I was right. It was!

NEW BRIDE

CRY

The journey home from Scotland was a real nightmare. I was as sick as a pig with my pregnancy, and I never want to see a Ritz Cracker dipped in Lime Marmalade ever again. We made our way from Liverpool over to my Auntie Pat's, where my Mum and Dad, along with my siblings, had de-camped to, in order that Mike's Mum couldn't harass them about where we'd run off? to. Auntie Pat had very kindly made her son, Tony, (who was about the same age as Mike and I) give up his single bed for our 'wedding night'. All made a huge fuss when it was time to go to bed, with lots of winking and digging Mike in the ribs, telling us to "keep the noise down" etc etc. I was mortified. I remember that Tony's bed squeaked dreadfully, so that even though we definitely WEREN'T doing anything, every time we even breathed, it sounded like we were 'AT IT' like rabbits, as the bed would groan underneath us. The following morning, there was much humor and mirth about Mike and I having a good night. We were mortified. If only they knew. I'd have seen more action if I'd have been in bed with a 'Mike' doll, 'Barbie's' man! (At least the 'immoveable' description matches!)

First thing on the following morning's agenda was to tell Mike's Mum. She was working as a temporary Manager at a Pub in Market Street, and Mike and I went to the phone box at the bottom of Auntie Pat's road. When he rang her, she hung up on him, refusing to believe he was now married, and to that 'harlot' who had got knocked-up by her little boy. Mike rang back and she started crying. He told her we would come to the Pub that morning and see her, but when we arrived, she wouldn't even look at me, but said, with her pointy witch's finger, all brown from smoking, "I'll give it 3 months". Meanwhile my Mum and Dad were offered a lovely house in The Meadow, on the Woodchurch Estate, so Mike and I moved in there with my 5 siblings and my parents. I remember that I would make up the pram with the lovely pram set, a lemon padded cover and pillow set (Back then, you didn't know if you were having a girl or a boy, so it was always safe to buy lemon, for either!) that I had bought in the Market, and I would push it up and down the street and around the bock, proud as punch. With Mike now living with us, my Dad had to stop his little games and my Mum hers, although her capacity for mental torture was still at its height. But I was a grown up now and they couldn't hurt me anymore. I became addicted to curry and chips as my pregnancy progressed and we'd all laugh that the baby would come out yellow like a Chinaman, as I ate it at least once every day. This could be seen by my blossoming weight. I was ten stone something beforehand, but not long after we'd got married, I was now up to over eleven stone. However, staying with Mum and Dad was still something of a problem. As I got bigger, I wasn't able to do as much around the house as Mum would have liked, so she took to waiting for Dad to come home from work, then bitch about me being 'lazy' and not

CRY

helping her out (it was SHE who was the lazy one!) so after asking Mike's Mum, we moved upstairs into the Pub. We had one room in the two-bedroom flat. I was still getting really sick every day, and as Christmas approached, I went to the Health Clinic and asked to be induced. On Christmas Eve morning, of 1968, I was admitted to Grange Mount Maternity Hospital, and after being given a foul potion of olive oil and orange juice to drink, the hospital Doctor broke my waters. This was quite a horrific experience for me at the time. Just having a man, albeit a Doctor, looking at your private parts in that way was a vile experience. I had previously been shaved by a nurse, and had had an enema, I then had to wait eight hours to see if my labor started on its own. It didn't, so a drip was pit in, and boy did my labor start with a vengeance. Only one of my four children were born without being induced, and the gentle start-up to labor without a drip is wonderful, as with the drip, the intense pains start almost immediately. During the night and into Christmas Day, I heard the nurse saying that it was snowing, but I couldn't have cared less. I was so high on the gas and air that whenever the nurse came in to check on me, I saw three of her. The pain was unbearable and I screamed out constantly. The nurses tried to get me to eat some spotted dick and custard, but I puked it all back up. Now, at just 16, I knew nothing about childbirth, but some weeks earlier, Mike and I had gone to see the movie 'Helga', in which she gives birth, all in close-up action. Naturally, never having come into contact with childbirth before, I was horrified and wanted to change my mind. So I kind of knew that it hurt, but boy, nothing prepared me for the pain like knives cutting you open. My Labor with Stephen was to last for twenty-seven hours. Then, at 6.40am on Christmas Day 1968, my son, Stuart Kenneth, was born. He didn't breathe for a few minutes but the wonderful staff soon worked their magic. I had a son. I had to keep saying it to myself. I had, for the past nine months, thought we would have a girl, Nicola, but here I was. I had a son. As it was Christmas Day, the hospital doctor and his family came in and gave me a lovely gift set of Bunnykins cutlery. Mike was allowed to stay for Christmas Dinner, and even his witch of a mother came in and said "Oh, He does look like our Mike, doesn't he?"!! Yes love, that's because he IS your Mike's!!

I was sent home with Stuart after a week. A first-time Mum at 16. I tried to breast feed him at first, but only managed, I think, about two months before putting him on the bottle. Mike and I started to look for a place of our own. His Mother was an absolute nasty piece of work, and would get him when he came home from work (He'd got an apprenticeship at Spillers Flour Mills on the Docks in Wallasey) and 'report' all my wrong-doings from that day to him. I would listen outside the door, then when she was in full flow, I would storm in, give her a filthy look and tell Mike to come into our room, where I would ask him, time after time, why he would never stick up for me. Mike's personality, as our marriage had come out of the 'honeymoon' stage,

CRY

(were we ever even in one? I don't think so!) was the same as it had always been, and worried me terribly. What on earth had I done? Sure, I didn't want the sex side of marriage, but I would have put up with it for the sake of being happy. But Mike was like a block of stone. He barely said a word, didn't take much interest in Stephen, and even less interest in me, and was just always in the background (where he would remain until 50 years later). When Stuart was about 6-8 weeks old, I have no idea why, but I once again 'cajoled' Mike into having sex. I still felt nothing, no enjoyment, nor did I have any feelings 'down there' whatsoever, but I had found out, within weeks of our marriage, that Mike was addicted to Pornography, and 'self-love', and had been since he was 12. No wonder he didn't want me when he had himself. Yet again, we had another 'go' when Stuart was about 6-8 weeks old. It was quite hard to try and get Mike to have sex. You could say he was never a big fan! Again, I have no explanation as to why I 'persuaded' him to have sex. I can only assume that it was the affection or love, whatever, that went with sex, that I so badly craved. Only I didn't get any of it with him. Never. So, this time, although I certainly didn't want it, neither did he, but the end result was that I got pregnant again. At first I didn't know it. I went into hospital, as my periods had returned, but were very erratic, and I was to have a curette (or D & C). After been shaved and gowned, the Doctor himself came to my bed and pulled the curtains round.

"I'm sorry to have to tell you Mrs. Ollman, but you're about 6 weeks pregnant!"

TRISH OLLMAN

My first thought was "Oh my God, we're going to have to tell his Mum that we've done 'it' again! I was sent home with instructions to go and see my Doctor, who later confirmed that Mark would arrive in about 7-months-time. Unbelievable that after only the second-time Mike and I had sex, I found myself, at not yet 17, to be pregnant again. I have asked myself over and over, why on earth did I never get pregnant with all of the other boys/men I'd had sex with? None of them had ever used any kind of protection, so why now? It remains, to this day, a mystery, and was to set the course for the rest of my unhappy life.

After looking for a place of our own for months, we had been offered a really old terraced house in Peel Street, Tranmere. It was really run down, and the mold everywhere was making us ill. Mark was only about 6 weeks old so we decided to go back to The Angel, but before we made the move back, an incident happened which nearly saw us lose our precious second son. I was working as a barmaid in the Pub on the corner of Peel Street, The Lord Raglan, and one evening, Mike came into the Pub to tell me that Mark, who would have been about 6 weeks old, had been taken to hospital. He had sustained a head injury. That's all I knew. I quickly asked the boss if I could leave early and got the bus to Birkenhead Children's Hospital, where my baby had been taken. While we waited to see him, a policeman had come and told me that Mike had, in a fit of rage because Mark wouldn't stop crying, had hit the baby on the head with his hand, on which

CRY

he had a signet ring. It was the signet ring that had caused the damage to Martin's head. Luckily it was not too serious, Mark just had a massive black eye, but we weren't allowed to take him home. I remember going up to the hospital every day for over a month to see my baby. Mike was not charged, but Social Services became involved with us and told us that until we got a place of our own and were settled, and I could prove that there would be no further incidents with Mike's temper. I was to find out that I never could curb his temper, but at the time, how did Social Services expect us to prove that, I wonder? But until they were satisfied with this young family (we were just 17) Mark had to say in the hospital. Therefore, even though I hated Mike's Mum with a passion, we had no option but to move back to the Pub. But again, Social Services intervened, and deemed that living above a pub did not make for a stable family home, so Mark was to stay in hospital for even longer. Naturally I was beyond distraught. I wanted my baby, and even at this early stage of our marriage, hated the bastard that had done this to him. At the Pub, there would now have been four of us living in the one bedroom, had Mark have been allowed home. We had had our names down on the Council Housing List for over a year. One day, with Mark still in the hospital, a lady from the Council came around out of the blue, and offered us a brand new two bedroom Flat on the Noctorum Estate, near Arrow Park in Birkenhead. This was a brand new Estate so I was over the moon. The next day, we got the bus and went to have a look at it. It was so new that there was still no letterbox in the door, but it did have something I had never seen before, and which greatly impressed me. There were two round sinks in the kitchen. I imagine back then that these flats would have been state of the art. It really was gorgeous. Various members of the family gave us bits of furniture (We had a couch where one side had to be held up by Stuart's plastic ride-on bus!) and we moved in that week. Every night we were there, before I went to bed, I would stand looking at it, not believing it was ours. And best of all, Mark was allowed to come home. Social Services soon disappeared, as they could see what good care I (alone I might add!) took of Stuart, and I was the happiest I had been in a long time. Mike was still not interested in sex, or me and the boys in the slightest, but at least we were all together. By now, I was used to Mike barely saying a word, and not playing with the boys, not doing the usual husbandly and fatherly things that most newly married men do, and he basically kept himself to himself, something that did not fit in well with my gregarious nature! (I was to learn over our \

50-year marriage that he would never change. It was always down to ME to leave him. So why didn't I? $1000 for anyone who can answer that question! I was still finding pornography under cushions and under the bed, but for the moment, it suited me not to be having sex. I was getting my love and adoration from my two wonderful, beautiful boys, whom I doted on. I was determined to be the mother to them that my own had not been to me. But my happiness was to be short

CRY

lived. One day, out of the blue, we received a letter through our new letterbox. It was a Notice of Eviction. It was from the Council Housing Department, and gave us 14 days to move out. I dressed the boys (Mike was at work at Spillers) and put them in the pram then went down to the town center on the bus and into the Housing Department to find out what this was all about. It turned out that someone had 'dobbed us in' to the Council for having lived for those few weeks in that old Peel Street house. I had no idea who this could have been, as we didn't have many friends. My only thought was that maybe it was one of the Pub patrons, who, through Mike's Mum, knew every minute of our lives. At the Council, even after I had explained how we'd barely been at Peel Street for only a few weeks, the Clerk was most unsympathetic and told me that as we hadn't 'declared' Peel Street to the Council, we had broken their rules and out we must go! I appealed and stamped my foot, but nothing would move them. Our gorgeous new flat was to become a distant memory!

There was no way whatsoever that I was going back to live with Mike's Mum (I must mention at this stage that his Dad was one of the loveliest men I've ever known, kind and gentle and quite a good friend to me. He also loved the boys and would play with them during his breaks from the Pub, but he was brow-beaten by his mean-mouthed wife and died of cancer far too young.) So, one of the other tenants near our new flat, whom I'd got friendly with suggested that I contact various charities (She was a Church-goer and gave me some names!) The second one I contacted, luckily, had a terraced house in Holbourn Hill, Tranmere, that members of the Church were doing up. When I explained our circumstances, the girl on the other end of the phone was almost in tears and told me that, of course, we could have that if we wanted it. The house was a typical two-up two-down brick terrace, but it had just had a new kitchen put in and a bathroom added by the Church. The rent was two pounds fifty a week, quite high in 1970, especially when Mike was only earning not quite six pounds a week, still a junior wage for a 17-year old. So, with no other option, we moved in there with the two boys, who were both under two years old. Mike, a smoker since he was eleven, would often walk the long distance to work at Spillers Flour Mills in the docks, from Holbourn Hill, instead of getting the bus, in order to buy a few 'penny-loose' cigarettes, as we were so poor that a pack of cigarettes for him wasn't even at the bottom of the list. He would often take what little money I had to buy us tea, out of my purse, and buy his dirty magazines, or cigarettes, causing me to fly into fits of anger. I paid many visits to the Citizens Advice Bureau for hand-outs just so we could eat, or put a shilling in the electric meter. One day, Mike came home from work at lunchtime, and I, a bored out of my brain housewife, persuaded him (easy!) to have the afternoon off. I sent him down to the garage at the end of the street to cash a two pound cheque, even though we didn't have two pounds in the bank (it was easier to become overdrawn with your bank back then). With

CRY

the two quid, we put a pound's worth of petrol into our old car (I'd sold the boys pram and with the money had paid five pounds for a Renault Dauphine from the Motor Auctions) and we set off, excited (well I was anyway! Not sure about Mike, Stuart and Mark, as it had started to rain!) to Rhyl in North Wales, about an hour's drive away. Once there, it was pouring with rain, so all we could do was to find a Café, where we both had egg and chips, and some chips for the boys and a 'cuppa' each. This feast took up every last penny we had so, with nothing else to do in the pouring rain, (I had hoped to take the boys to the beach), we set off back home. But just outside Rhyl, our windscreen wipers broke. Luckily, we were on the outskirts of Rhyl and not yet in the countryside, and Mike, in the pouring rain, managed to drive the car, almost at a snail's pace, in the pouring rain, with no wipers, a hundred meters to, thankfully, a garage. There we were told the wiper motor had gone and that it would cost twenty-five pounds to fix. That was a month's wages for us, so there was absolutely no option of getting it fixed. The man in the Garage took pity on us and knew of our long journey home, back to Birkenhead, so went and fetched his mop. He sawed half of the handle off and gave it to me to keep the windscreen reasonably clear of rain for Mike to see through. What a sight we must have been: clapped out old car, two crying boys in the back, Mike with his head over the steering wheel, peering out of the windscreen so he could just see through the rain, and me, side window open, and my arm soaking wet, as I used the half a mop to keep wiping the windscreen so that we could get home. The upside (yes, there is one) to this, is that Mike and I have never laughed so much in all of our lives. A rare event, indeed.

Our time living in Holbourn Hill seemed to be one of poverty, of never having enough money and living hand-to-mouth every week. We existed mostly on liver and onions or sausages. Mike and his parents had eaten lots of 'hogge' and tripe (pigs and cow's stomachs), as well as heart and, to me unheard of, rabbits. So, he didn't care what we had, and left it to me to do the shopping and decide what we ate. One day, Mike's sister, Susan, had just had a large chest freezer, something I'd never seen before, as they were very new, and as part of the package she'd taken out, it was filled with meats and vegetable and other frozen foods, an absolute luxury to me who could only ever afford the cheapest of cheap meat, mainly liver. Two days before pay day, I went around to where Susan and her family lived, as I usually did most days. The boys were playing with her two youngest children, and I was very aware that not only did I have absolutely no money, but I also had no food in for tea that night. So, when Susan nipped up to the toilet, I quickly went to the freezer, took out the first thing that came to hand, and put it in my bag. When I got home, I found out what my stolen spoils was. It was liver. Yes, of course I feel ashamed at stealing food from my own family, but when you have children that you can't feed, all

CRY

sense of right and wrong goes out of the window. Doesn't it?

One Christmas Eve, during our nearly three years in Holbourn Hill, I left Mike with the boys and went down to the old Birkenhead Market to get the last few things for the following day for the boys. When I went to pay for two Selection Boxes, my first purchase, I realized I didn't have my purse. Assuming it had been stolen, I went to the Police Station by the Town Hall to see if anyone (unlikely but you never know!) had handed it in. But no, nobody had. I was beyond upset and mortifies. No money and Christmas tomorrow. I hadn't yet bought any food for Christmas Dinner and the boys still only had a few cheap things each. I explained to the policeman that the money in my purse was for food a few things for Christmas for my boys, so he advised me once again go to the Citizen's Advice Bureau. When I arrived there, (their office was in Hamilton Square,) a few minutes from the Police Station, the lady was just about to close up for the holidays. When I told her my sorry tale, she took a cashbox out of her draw and opened it. There was twelve pounds in it (two week's wages for us!) and said "This if the Lord Mayor's Emergency Fund. Here, take it, and have a happy Christmas". I was stunned. I'd never had so much money in my entire life before. I headed straight back to the Market and bought those Selection Boxes, plus a few little toy cars for the boys, and a pen (Why he never wrote a word?) for Mike. I then headed to Tesco's, a small supermarket, on Grange Road, and bought a turkey. Now, you have to realize, that even though I knew turkeys were a Christmas thing, I, nor my family, had ever had one. Mum had always cooked the once-a-year chicken for Christmas Day all my life. It was the only day we got chicken and we thought it 'special'. I also got a box of stuffing and a few other goodies which we wouldn't have normally had. With two heavy bags to get home. I then did something previously unheard of; I got a Taxi home. The look on Mike's face when I walked through the door with the two laden bags from Tesco's was a picture. "Where did you get all that from?". I told him my purse had been stolen and of the generosity of the Citizen's Advice Bureau. He turned around, and from the table picked up my purse! Yes, it had not been stolen at all. I'd left it at home. What an idiot I felt. I vowed to pay back the CAB after Christmas. But did I? No, of course I didn't. Where the heck would I have got twelve quid from!!

With the boys now toddlers, and desperate for more money to make ends meet, I got a job as an Operator for a Taxi firm, and while Mike worked during the day and I looked after the boys, at night, it was me who went out to work. I soon found a job (Gee, how easy was it to find work back in the late sixties and early seventies?) as a Radio Operator for a Taxi Firm, located just a short distance from the Old Birkenhead Market. Almost immediately, I, at 19 years old, caught the eye of Barry, whose Taxi call-sign was 'Baker 3'. After a few weeks of him 'chatting me up', Barry

CRY

started taking me home at around 1am each morning when the office closed. Now, old habits die hard, so they say, and we were soon having sex in the back of his car. I say 'we' were having sex, but yet again, I was just the block of wood, allowing him to do what it is that a man having sex do. This was the first man I had been with since marrying Mike, and I have to admit, it felt good to be 'wanted' by Barry, held in his arms, and listening to him telling me how beautiful I was. I'm not silly. I'm sure he only said those things as a bit of 'petting' and, as he would have thought, to 'get me in the mood', but he had no idea of my distaste for sex. No, it wasn't just a distaste, it was an actual fear of it, so much so that I wanted to run a mile, just as I always had. I'm angry now that I once again allowed myself to be used by a man who was much older than me, and whom I didn't particularly like. I'd never 'fancied' a boy or a man all my life and didn't know what it felt like to do so, nor why women could also enjoy the sex act. It was completely foreign to me. Anyway, after he had finished with me, he was to again ask me "How come you never come"? As I'd done in the past, I had said "Oh, I did". Whenever asked that question, as I had been a few times over the years, I had never understood what it meant, but this time I did. Mike had brought home some pornographic comics when he'd worked at Spillers, and one day when he was out at work, I had had a sneak-peak at them. I found their content absolutely vile and wondered what on earth Mike could see in them, and, get such pleasure from. I found them to be tawdry and offensive and was to wonder, yet again, why Mike would prefer 'loving' himself to having me, the real thing. I can say, without bragging, that I was a good-looking girl, I had a great figure and lovely shoulder length shiny hair. I asked Mike about the magazines and comics and he told me he'd got them from a man who worked on the docks, which I suppose is where he got all his pornography from. So, by the time I was being driven home by Barry, I must have had some knowledge of what it meant, but still I always lied and said I had 'come'. I knew of the word 'orgasm' but of course, had no idea how one had one or what it felt like. So, I just lied as usual to Barry. One evening, Mike must have suspected something, as, late that night, and leaving our two small boys alone asleep at home, he walked down to near the old Birkenhead Market, where the Taxi firm was, and stood across the road in the darkness. Now because it was late, I would always keep the front door locked, so if a driver ever wanted to come back to base, he would knock and I would go and open the door and let him in. This night, Barry came back to Base to see me, as he usually did. We'd been having our 'Affair for about a month now and his lust for me (as that was all it was. He was a married man!) still wasn't abating. I opened the door and he took me in his arms and kissed me, showering me with words of love, whispering to me what he wanted to 'do to me' later. Even though I knew the dreaded sex act would surely follow, I drank in his words like nectar, just as I had back when I was 13, when I had got similar words from boys or men in the back alleys, the back of a car, in the cinemas, or in the railway carriage. This night, I was high on adrenalin. Barry wasn't an attractive man but he certainly wasn't ugly either and I looked forward to finishing work in an hour or two. It was then that I spotted Mike standing across the road in the shadows, watching what was happening. I have no memory of what happened after that, other than Mike never said a single word about it. Barry and I quickly went through to the office and the next time I looked Mike had gone. When I got home that night, Mike was already asleep in bed and the incident was never mentioned. But as I lay unable to sleep, I realized it had to stop. I was older now and could think more rationally. I was a married woman, albeit without a 'husband', but I had my boys to love me and for me to love them. I decided that night that as soon as the boys were older, I would leave Mike, and live alone with them. Men just weren't for me! I gave up the Taxi job shortly afterwards, and never saw Barry again. It had never been 'an affair' or any kind of 'relationship' between myself and Barry, it was just free sex with an attractive young girl who couldn't say no to him, just as I had never been able to say No" to anyone since I'd been 13. Anyway, I'm pretty sure Mike had just been curious as he never, ever mentioned it and life went on as normal. But inside me, an almighty change happened that night. From now on, I was no man's sex toy.

Having let Men use me as a sexual object was all part and parcel of my damaged personality, both by my parents and then by Mike. I was the girl first, then the young woman, that I had become, from past abuse, and being used for sex by boys and men who happened into my life at various times. I was so used to it after so many years, but I still, for some unknown reason, couldn't, and still can't to this very day, understand why Mike preferred to use his pornography instead of using me. I was quite an attractive young girl, with lovely thick hair and a good figure, even after having the babies. I would still find the porn everywhere, often 'the worse for wear' and the fighting started. Well, when I say fighting, it was more of a one-way shouting match by me. Mike would just take it, occasionally rolling his eyes, shrug his shoulders. He really, really, didn't care one iota what me or his children, or his family, thought about him. He was oblivious to everything around him, and the world could go fuck itself for all he cared. He had his pornography and masturbation, along with his ciggies, and life was all rosy for him. He's still like that to this day. So when I started shouting, absolutely in frustration, at him and him saying nothing back, this only increased my frustrations more. We would have the occasional bit of sex over the years, ALWAYS initiated by me (Why?? Again, I just don't understand. I HATED sex so why even bother. Maybe I saw him as a bit if a challenge? I am a traditionalist, and believe in the ideals of marriage and all that it entails. I was brought up a strict Catholic, so maybe I felt it was my 'duty', I have no idea, but neither of us enjoyed it. As it was always me who had to make the first move when

CRY

we were in bed, I began to resent it. Why? Because I badly wanted another baby, a girl, and I think that was the reasoning behind my occasionally 'tempting' him. Over time, Mike had lost his job, firstly Spillers, then at Cammel Laird's, and we had been on the dole, hiding behind the couch when the rent man came, for about a year.

Just before Christmas of 1972, the Government decided that everyone on the dole had to accept work wherever they could find it in England, or they would lose their weekly benefits. The Job Center could only find Mike a job hundreds of miles away in the small seaside town of Hearn Bay, in Kent, as a Pallet Maker, and he had no option but to take it. And so, on 5th January 1973, Mark's third birthday, Mike packed a suitcase and went down to Kent on the train, not only to start his new job, but to also find us somewhere to live. But after a week, he had phoned (Yes, we had obtained a red Bakelite phone by now) to say that there was absolutely nothing to rent in Hearne Bay. Unbelieving, I decided to pack up our small house by myself and travel down there with the boys. Surely, I thought, I would be able to find us somewhere. Mike just hadn't looked properly! The deal back then with the Government, was that if you couldn't find anywhere permanent to live, they would hold your furniture and effects in storage until you did. So that's what happened. A large removal van turned up the day we were due to leave Birkenhead, and took our things away to a storage unit (I later found out they were stored in London). Because I wasn't close to any of my family, and by this time my two brothers had also moved out of home and were working in different parts of the country, there were no goodbyes. My parents were on the brink of Divorce and I didn't want to say farewell to them anyway.

Myself and our two young boys arrived, by train, in Hearne Bay one cold and rainy Friday afternoon. Mike met us at the Station and told us that we could stay at quite a good Hotel, the only one he'd been able to find which had a room big enough available. I found this to be very peculiar indeed, as Hearne Bay is a seaside resort and must have had lots of Hotels. But we made the short trip to the chosen Hotel in a taxi. It was early evening, and after feeding the boys, I put them to bed. Now, you would expect any normal man, who hasn't seen his young wife in a week to be quiet, well, you know, keen. So, I had a shower (something new for me as we only ever had a sink, and more recently, a bath!) put on a spray or two of the only cheap perfume I owned, and got into bed. Mike didn't even make use of the shower, just peed, then got into bed with his T-Shirt on, turned over, and said goodnight then went to sleep. Now you'd think after just over 4 years of marriage, I would be used to the constant rejection by him. I hadn't gone out searching for another man again, as you know by now that I wasn't interested in men in the slightest. But by this time in our marriage, even though I didn't want the sex, I did want the loving and the closeness that all happy couples should have.

CRY

I had told Mike often that I would be happy to have sex with him just so that we could enjoy some intimacy, and perhaps have that much-wanted baby girl, but it fell on deaf ears. He just wasn't interested. He had his porn, now a long-standing addiction, as well as his 'self-loving' (I HATE the other word for it!) and he wasn't interested in me and my nubile young body in the slightest. You'd think I would be used to this rejection by now. But I wasn't. It made my heart ache. Why was I not worthy to him, when I'd been more than worthy before I'd married him? I could have gone out and had an affair at any point (I did have a bit of a 'dalliance' once, with Barry from the Taxi's, if you remember?) but even though I never had any enjoyment from sex itself, I did crave the attention, along with the associated affection that came with being wanted, even if I do now realize that the words said to me where just that: words to get me allow a boy or man to have sex. I had it in my mind now, not realizing what I came to know much later, that Ian certainly didn't love me in any way whatsoever. He only ever loved one person, and that person was himself. So, laying wide awake in that expensive bed, in that expensive room, in that expensive Hotel, I cried my eyes out.

The following day, a Saturday, and Mike had to work until 1pm at the pallet makers. It was now my job to find us somewhere to live. I got dressed, dressed the boys and packed the few belongings I had brought with us from Birkenhead. The Hotel Manager was a lovely middle aged man, who said I could leave the bags behind the Hotel desk, while I went into town to look for somewhere to live. The sea front along Hearne Bay was bitterly cold (It was January, the middle of the English winter) and I walked almost to the top, Mark in a pushchair and Stuart walking beside me, holding onto the pram. When we reached the small main street I immediately spotted an Estate Agents. However, I was to be disappointed. They had nothing to rent, indeed there WAS nothing to rent in the whole town, I was told. All of the Boarding Houses were full of Students waiting to go back to college in Canterbury and the lady behind the counter told me that there was absolutely nothing. There being no other Estate Agents in the town, I had no option but to go into the various shops and ask if they knew of anything to rent. The answer was always the same. So, it was with a heavy heart, and tears streaming down my cheeks, that I made my way back up the Sea Front and back to the Hotel and our luggage to wait for Mike to finish work at 1pm. To make matters worse, it had decided to start snowing. Sounds ethereal? No, just bitterly cold. The boys, seeing me cry, also started crying, so we were a sorry sight when we got back to the Hotel where our bags were behind the counter. There was no question of us staying there another night, as it was four pounds a night for a double room. I had brought seven pounds with me, and Ian had about a pound. But we had nowhere to live. Nowhere in Hearne Bay and nowhere back in Birkenhead. But someone was looking down on us that day. The

CRY

Manager of the Hotel we'd stayed at the night before and took pity on us. He told me he'd "ring around" everyone he knew and so it was that he found us an attic room with a single bed, in a Men's Boarding House at the top of the Sea Front. We waited in the Hotel for Mike to finish work, and together we all walked up to the Boarding House in the freezing snow. It was a narrow, but tall building, and our room was at the very top. The landlady was really kind and brought us up a camp bed for the boys to 'top and tail', while Mike and I had to make do with a single bed. We were told that a man was arriving in two weeks to live in the room but that we could have it until then.

The following day, a Sunday, and we walked all over Hearne Bay. Again, someone was watching over us, as we came across a house that obviously had nobody living in it. (Easily spotted, as it had no curtains up to the window.) It was a terraced house at number 6 Banks Street, and I knocked next door to ask about it, but was told it was Council property and had been condemned for eight years. We walked back to the Boarding House and, I know I did, I had it at the back of my mind that we would squat in it if we couldn't find anything else by the time came when we had to leave our present room. We stopped off at a shop, and with the last of our money, bought a tin of Fray Bentos Pie, a tin of peas, and a tin of those awful boiled yellowing potatoes. With the few pence we had left, we bought the boys a few sweets each. That was it. We were broke, and it was only Sunday. Mike didn't get paid until the following Friday, and we had to be out of the Boarding House by first thing the following Saturday week. The next day, Monday, Mike went to work, and I put Mark in the pushchair, Stuart only a year older, holding onto the pram handle, and we walked the seven miles to Canterbury, where we found the Social Security office. I told them of our plight and I can't remember how much they gave me, but we managed, just, until pay day. The seven-mile walk back, was a breeze. I had money in my purse again. I was happy, on the outside, at least.

Throughout the two weeks, we kept looking for somewhere to live, but there was nothing, and I think we both knew that the derelict house in Banks Street was going to be our only hope. On the last Friday night there, Mike and I lay in our single bed, and with no other option, decided that he would call in sick at work the following morning, and then 'break into' the house in Banks Street. After a pretty much sleepless night, the next morning, we got dressed and packed up our belongings, thanked the landlady who wished us good luck, and made our way to Banks Street, where our plan was for me and the boys to stand and wait at the top of the Street, and for Mike to go and try and break in somehow. To my amazement, he was back within moments. The front window was unlocked and all he had to do was to lift it to gain entry. We all almost ran there, but there was an obstacle: As the house had been empty for eight years, there was eight years' worth of junk mail which had been put through the

CRY

letterbox, making it impossible to open the front door. Mike had to go over to the shop and get some large bags to clear away all the hundreds of Pools Coupons and brochures and other such detritus. Once cleared, we could explore the rest of the house. As I said earlier, the neighbor had told me that the house was condemned. We were to see why. Climbing up the stairs, I fell through a step. Upstairs, large parts of the roof tiles were missing and the sky could be seen through the holes. There was mold and cobwebs everywhere. Back downstairs, there was an overgrown rear concrete yard and an outside toilet, which had no water in, and was orange with rust. When Mike pulled on the chain, it come away in his hand. Back inside the small kitchen, we tried to see if there was, by chance, any hot water. Are you in the slightest bit surprised that there was no water at all. In fact, the only livable room was the front one which had relatively escaped the ravages of the rest of the house. That was Ok, I thought, but without conviction. We'd all live in there. Surely, we'd get a Council House soon if they saw us all living like this? So, I rang the Removal Company and asked how quickly they could deliver out furniture etc. That afternoon be Ok? Sure, that would be great. Next job was to go to the phone box and ring the electricity and gas people. I couldn't ring the council about there being no water, as they would then know we were squatting in one of their derelict properties, so I thought I'd ask the lady next door if I could fill a couple of pans up with her water, which she kindly allowed me to do. "You can't live in there, especially with them little ones" she offered her advice. "How about we all come and move in with you?" I almost asked her! First came the gas man. He took one look at his clipboard. "This place is condemned. If I try and put the gas on it would probably blow the whole place sky high" he told me. Sorry, but he "couldn't do it!" Ok. I can work with no gas. Half an hour later, the electric man arrived. "This place is condemned. If I was to try and turn on any power it would probably blow the place up! What are you doing here anyway? We have this house as condemned on our books." Ok. So now I have a problem. But ever tenacious, we went out to the Chandlers shop and bought oil lamps and a small camping stove with a blue gas bottle. Unfortunately, the oil lamps just spewed thick black smoke into the room, so Mike went back and bought some candles. When the Removal van arrived that afternoon, it had been snowing all day and the house was freezing, as we had no heating. The poor driver and his mate unloaded all of our things into the front room and the moldy back room. The driver was almost in tears. "You can't stay here," he said. But we had no choice. I told him our story and, upset, he gave me a pound note. So 6 Banks Street was our new home and, the four of us living in just one room, we'd be there for four months.

Back then, if you moved to another part of the UK for work (otherwise they would stop your dole!) once you'd been in the new place for a month, you got the almighty sum of four hundred pounds as a 're-

CRY

settlement' payment. The day our cheque arrived, Mike and I danced around the little front room as if we'd become millionaires. It was more money that we had ever seen in either of our lives, an absolute fortune. We had been slowly selling off bits of furniture and some of the larger of the boy's toys, in order to survive, as Mike's wages were very low, with him still being so young. The only thing I was cooking on the little one ring camp stove was soup, tinned spaghetti, or Baked Beans. The rest of the time we went to the Chip Shop on the corner. We had a bucket which we used as a pee toilet, especially at night, and used the Public Toilets in the park around the corner. You had to put a penny in the slot before the door would open. The lady next door was lovely and kept us with water. Even though it was winter, and the 'off-season' there was one Amusement Arcade open on the sea front, and with the boys playing on the motorized animals, I would play 'Prize Bingo' on most days. (No wonder we never had any money!) How we managed to survive four months in that house I will never know, but it's amazing what you do when you're young and in the face of adversity. By the time we had been there for four months, we only had about fifty pounds left out of the four hundred Government Re-Settlement Grant. Mike spotted an Ad in our local paper, that an Estate of brand new houses was being built, about twenty miles away, and you could buy one with just fifty pounds deposit. There was an 'Open House' showing time advertised for 6pm the following day. We were very excited at the thought of owning our own home, and desperate to move out of our hovel in Banks Street, so the next day, after Mike had finished work, I had dressed the boys nicely, made an effort with myself, and having already found out where the bus went from, we made our way to the seafront to make the journey. Surely, this was the break we very much needed that would change our lives?

NEW BEGINNINGS?

It had been about a year since my 'relationship' with Barry and the Taxi Company. It had been with real determination that, as I certainly didn't like, or want sex, and my little boys fulfilling my need for love, I never went near another man. Not only did I, luckily, never really had the opportunity since, but I made sure I avoided any situation where I might be alone with a man. But as the time went on, and remember, I was

CRY

still only about 19, still an attractive girl, and even though we had no money, I kept myself looking as best as I could in the hope (WHY?? It was NEVER going to happen) that Mike would 'come around' and become a 'proper' husband to me. But no. There was absolutely NOTHING there for him. He barely interacted with the boys and said only the very basic necessities to me. But I still wanted a baby girl. I was going to call her Nicola Jane, and would daydream about her, all the time in pretty pink dresses. So yes, every now and then, I would basically almost force Mike into having sex. He found it hard to get an erection and when he did, our lovemaking was soon over, He never, ever, spoke any words of affection to me and time after time, I would lay crying afterwards as he slept (He could sleep on a plank of wood in two minutes flat if necessary!) It was natural that I often thought about leaving him. But where could I go? I had no money, no family that I could stay with, so, life went on. It seemed that in order to gain Mike's attention, I would have had to have dyed my hair blond, have a boob job, and get myself into a porn magazine, for him to become excited over me!

About a year or so ago, while we were still living in Holbourn Hill, in Birkenhead, prior to moving down to Kent, we had seen a poster in the local train station, advertising an Australia Day Expo. As was the British attitude in the early 70s, Australia was seen as a Mecca, a place of year-round sunshine and wealth. Kangaroos and those cute Koalas on every corner. Big blue skies and white sandy beaches. Oh, what a life you could live over there. Did I want a piece of that? You bet I did! The Expo was to be held on the following Sunday in a Hall in Manchester. Living in such poverty and under the constant grey skies of Birkenhead, Mike and I thought we'd go along and see what you had to do to live over there. We were totally fed-up with life as it was, and having no close relatives that we would miss, we became quite excited by the idea. The following Sunday, we caught a train to Manchester with the boys, excited at the thought of living in Australia. In each corner of the big hall there was a Display by each of the Australian States. New South Wales, Queensland, Victoria, South Australia, Tasmania, Western Australia and the Northern Territory. Each State's Display had a trestle table, an Australian flag hung on the wall, as well as their own State flags, along with photos, new and old, some localized History, and a charming young lady tantalizing you to choose her State to emigrate to. We were immediately drawn to the New South Wales Display, as it had a COLOUR TV showing 'Life Down Under'. We stood watching in awe and amazement as the Port Kemble Steelworks were shown as shiny silver (in reality they are black, and the footage shown must have been taken years ago when brand new!) and what we then knew as 'rich' people's houses, 'Bungalows' or single story houses, which were the norm in Australia. On the screen, we saw pictures of these houses with, also previously unseen, long, grassy gardens, (We'd only even known concrete back

CRY

yards). Cut to neighbors talking over the fence, and then, the highlight. Something that made me want to go and live in Australia over all else, there before our eyes, was footage of two young couple, a few children playing with a ball amongst all that grass, and the man wore, of all things, AN APRON! If that wasn't shocking in itself, there was a contraption called, we were being told, a Bar-B-Que and it had MEAT cooking on it. And not liver or sausages, but something called 'Steak'. This was what life in New South Wales could offer us, the young lady behind the stand told us. We were gobsmacked. Of course, we'd seen the odd bit of meat, and lots of liver, but steaks the size of your hand? But hang on. How on earth would we cook egg and chips on that contraption? I naively asked the young female attendant of the Stall, who laughed and said that we probably wouldn't be eating egg and chips if we were to emigrate to NSW. Of course, I wanted to go. Desperately. A new life. That was just what I needed. I wasn't getting any love or excitement from Mike. In fact, I was still getting NOTHING from him whatsoever. Our house, if it hadn't been for the noise the boys made, would have been like a mausoleum! (Although I knew he existed and was not a figment of my imagination, as I was still regularly finding his pornography under cushions and under the bed!) Anyway, we filled-in the Application Forms there and then, along with the hundreds of other hopefuls, and were encouraged to ask questions. (I asked if I would still be able to use my iron!) We were told that if Australia House thought us suitable for Emigration, we would be called for Interview in about a month. Before we left, Mike had picked up a brochure depicting the same Steel Works we had just seen on the Screen. It appeared that they were offering to sponsor young families like ours, and allow their men to have a job to go to upon our arrival. Mike filled that form in too, and handed it to the lady on the New South Wales Display stand. To our great excitement, about three weeks later, we received a letter in the Post asking us to go to Manchester the following week for an Interview to 'Emigrate to New South Wales, in Australia'. That form from the Steel Works in Wollongong which Mike had filled in when we had attended the Expo weeks earlier had paid off. We also received a blue 'Air Mail' letter where they offered to sponsor him and give him work as a laborer at a starting salary of $111 a week, (which at the time, would have been the equivalent of about seventy pounds, an absolute fortune). Back then, Mike's weekly wage was about nine pounds, so $111 seemed like we would be millionaires. Because of the Steel Works sponsorship, (Its full title was 'Australian Iron and Steel') we had been deemed suitable as Migrants and had been offered the Interview. At the Expo in Manchester, we had been told that if you were sent for a Medical, after your Interview, then you were almost certain to go. The Interview went well, although the man interviewing us must have thought Mike to be a mute, he barely said a word. (It's a wonder we passed!) Now you who know me will understand why I talk so much!! I've had to talk for two all my adult life! When the Interview, which consisted of questions about our background (naturally, I didn't give much away about mine!) was over, we were told we would be informed if we had passed through to have our Medicals – the final stage. (I've since found out that, in reality, we were the perfect Migrants. Two healthy boys, Mike, even with his problems, with a job to go to, and we were young, and more importantly, healthy – the Australian Government wouldn't take you if you had any health problems as it would have meant they would have had to pay your Health Care costs under their Medicare Scheme, similar to the NHS, and serious health problems would rule any applicants out as being 'a drain on the country'. (Mass Migration has made Australia into the country it is today, so I feel this rule to be very unfair. I'm not sure of policies today in 2020, but I do know from friends, that Australia is now a very difficult country to emigrate to.)

So here we are, back in Hearne Bay, fifty pounds in the bank and about to catch a bus to go and view a new housing development, a chance to become home owners. We were, by now, twenty, and had been married for over four years. We arrived at the bus stop, which was located on the sea front, only to find that we'd just missed the bus and the next one was an hour away. We had kind of put Australia to the back of our minds, as we hadn't heard anything from Australia House for so long. So to pass the time while we waited for the next bus, we decided to walk up the sea front to the Boarding House we had first stayed at, to see if any mail had come for us. Highly unlikely, as we didn't really ever get mail. As we entered the front door, there, on the hall table, was an official-looking letter addressed to Mr and Mrs Ollman. It had the Australian crest on the envelope. I tore it open and as it was so unexpected, I almost passed out. It was from Australia House telling us that we had been approved and that they would be in contact with us about having our Medical Examinations shortly. Naturally we forgot about the new housing development and went back to Banks Street, obviously elated. The following day, I rang Australia House in London, from the phone box, and gave them the Banks Street address so that we could be informed about when and where to have our Medicals. The lady there told us that Medicals were usually held about four to six weeks after the letter had been sent out. We were disappointed that we'd have to stay in Banks Street for that much longer, but we needn't have worried. A few days later we were to get the bad news in the post. The Council had found out that we'd been squatting there for four months, and gave us a 48-hour Eviction Notice. When I rang them, saying we had nowhere else to go, the boys and I were offered a place at a Refuge, but Mike had to find somewhere himself, or sleep on the streets. We had no option but to go back up to Birkenhead, and try and stay with a relative. But which one? There was nobody who we thought we wanted to stay with, but beggars can't be chooses, and, we thought, once we'd had our Medical, it would only be a matter of time before we took off for the other side of the world. So with nowhere to stay back in Birkenhead, I thought about

CRY

going over to New Brighton, a small resort town not far from Birkenhead, where I was sure we would easily find a B&B until I could find somewhere else for long enough until we'd passed our Medicals and had a date to go to Australia. As I'd thought, it had been easy. There were lots of B&B's to choose from in New Brighton and we soon found a cheap one. The following day, we looked in a Liverpool Newspaper for cheap rentals. The cheapest was a caravan in Prestatyn, North Wales, I rang up and arranged for us to take it on a weekly basis, as I didn't know how long Australia House would take. So that morning saw us on the move yet again. Before we left New Brighton, I again rang Australia House, giving my Mum's neighbor's phone number and address (My parents had divorced by now and Mum didn't have a phone) and once in Wales, we waited, in the caravan, for the letter with our Medical appointment to arrive. Stupidly, instead of saving what little money we had for Australia, we bought a small portable TV for the caravan, and, even though Mike got a temporary job at Pontins Holiday Camp as a Chalet Porter, (At that time, they were filming 'Holiday on the Buses', with Reg Varney and Wilfred Bramble – Steptoe - and if you ever get the chance to see that movie, in the ballroom scene, you can just see a young Stuart and Mark sitting on the floor at my feet. All of us 'extras' got paid: a can of soft drink each!) we still struggled to get by each week. This, of course, was not helped by the fact that I became addicted to the Arcade Bingo (I actually won a set of three suitcases, which we used when we left the UK) Very soon, there was nothing left of the four hundred pounds we'd got as a relocation allowance. I regularly rang Australia House (Yes, back in the day, they did have a Receptionist who answered your call. Not so today!) to see when we were getting our Medicals, as we knew that emigrating to that wonderful sunny land, where kangaroos hopped and cute little Koala's hugged you (Sure! Don't believe a word of it!) would shortly follow. One Sunday, we decided to take a trip on the bus to Chester, a lovely historic city in North West England. While we were there, I went to a phone box and rang my Mum's neighbor. To my absolute amazement, she told me that, yes, there was a letter from Australia House giving us a place, date and time to attend our Medical Appointments. It was just two weeks away and couldn't have come at a better time, as the caravan that we were renting, it's owner had said she needed it back for one of her own family. When I told her about the upcoming emigration, she very kindly agreed to let us stay on until we were leaving. The following week, I went into town and bought the boys new vests and underpants for the Medical, using almost the last of what money I had. I had to make a phone call and went to the phone box. A few minutes after ending the call and leaving the phone box, I remembered I had left the bag with the boys' new underwear in the phone box. I rushed back, and it would have been less than five minutes later, but alas, the bag with the underwear was gone. I was devastated, as going to a Doctor, and especially on such an important appointment as this

CRY

was, without new underwear, was a disaster. (It's a generational thing!) Eventually, the day of the Medical arrived, and we all took extra care getting washed and doing our hair. We got on the bus to Prestatyn where the Doctor was, unbelievably nervous, (well I was anyway, Mike never expressed any emotion whatsoever) and spent about an hour with the four of us getting our hearts, throats, blood pressure etc. checked. It's all a bit of a blur, but I can remember there was nothing difficult about it, and I had been worrying for no reason. The Doctor, a lovely elderly man, told us that we'd all passed with flying colors, much to my delight. This was it now, as far as I was concerned. We were all but there. Back at the bus stop, I was to get an almighty shock. I had lost my purse, with the wages Mike had only received from Pontins the day before. It was too far to walk back to the Caravan Park, so we had no option but to tell the Bus Conductor what had happened. He kindly let us on and we went back to the caravan to wait. Would we, or wouldn't we, be heading out of our miserable lives in England, and spending the rest of our days, 'Down Under'?

"I COME FROM THE LAND DOWN UNDER"

The wait seemed to take forever. I took to phoning my Mum's neighbor, Eileen, every few days to see if there was any news. If she got sick of me ringing, she never showed it, and was always kind and pleasant, apologetic if no letter had arrived. Then, One Sunday, I rang her. The excitement in her voice when she told me that a Telegram had arrived for us on Friday was palpable. She read it out to me:

"Would you prefer to travel to Australia by boat or plane? Please advise Australia House as soon as possible."

Wow! I couldn't believe it. I rushed back home to tell Mike and the boys, who were by now, almost four and five, then went back to the phone box to tell the owner of the caravan. The following day, Monday, realizing that we didn't have the necessary funds for a six-week boat trip, I rang Australia House and told them we would like to go by plane. I was told that a letter would be in the Post within the next few days with our tickets and flight instructions. We were going to a place called Wollongong, and would have accommodation in a Hostel, 'Fairy Meadow'. Can you imagine the feelings I had? 'Fairy Meadow'. To my ears, it sounded like Utopia, Mike gave his Notice into Pontins and we once again packed our belongings into the three new suitcases that I'd won at prize bingo weeks ago, two with all our clothes and the photo album I had, along with some toiletries, and the small third suitcase, with the boys' toy cars (which was, at the time, the only and

CRY

cheapest things I could spoil them with. They had dozens. – I still am a 'spoiler'!!) We then rang ahead and asked Mike's sister, Susan, if we could stay with her for two nights in Birkenhead until we left, and she agreed. When the acceptance letter had arrived, we were told that we needed a passport each and forty pounds (The Ten Pound Pom had, the year before, been replaced with The Twenty Pound Pom!) and we were travelling in three weeks. I hadn't given a thought to passports, so headed straight to the Post Office in Birkenhead, where, I was told, it usually took four to six weeks to get a new passport, but they would expedite our applications under the circumstances. Only problem was, that after paying for our rent and other bills, with Mike's wages from Pontins, we were twenty pounds short. No problem. I pawned my wedding ring (I had bought myself a second hand one from the Exmouth Street Pawn Shop a few years ago) and a bracelet my grandma had left me. I would do anything it took to get us 'Down Under'. A new life, a new start, that's what I needed. Once we were all settled, I would leave Mike and strike out with my two boys, on our own. I doubted if Mike would even miss us!

On the 10th June, 1973, we boarded our first ever plane, a Qantas 707 bound for Kingsford Smith Airport in Sydney, Australia. I can remember the Terminal at Heathrow being a small square building and inside, just one café and a 'Waiting Lounge', a far cry from how it is today, one of the world's major and largest airports. But back in 1973, not many people flew and the airport, although having been there for quite a long time, had not been developed o received the mass of passengers it has today. Soon enough, it was time to board, and Mark didn't want to get on this giant beast of a plane. But after a bit of persuasion with a few sweets, we boarded and were shown to our seats by a lovely looking young lady in a uniform and a hat. She was what was called (all new to us, obviously) our 'Air Hostess'. Of course we were excited. Taking off was scary for the boys but they soon settled down and enjoyed this big, new adventure for them. They were three and four and on their first ever plane. You will all know that the flight from the UK to Australia is unbelievably long. I think these days you can do it in about 22-23 hours, but in 1973 it took much longer. Never having been further than Kent in our lives, he boys started to get restless. Our Air Hostess had given them coloring books but there's only so much coloring a little one can be expected to do. So I got the little pillows and blankets and, as there was hardly anybody else on our flight, I asked the Air Hostess if we could use the empty rows of seats to sleep. She kindly told us, of course, we could, So I put each boy into a separate row, with a pillow and blanket and told that that if they went to sleep I would get them an ice cream when were in Australia, I'd previously tried to explain to them that Australia was a long way away (I'd shown them on a map) and that we were going to live there. I'd told them all, about the beautiful sand and the sea and all the kangaroos (Yeah, sure!) but I think

CRY

they were still too young to understand what was happening. Luckily, they did sleep, and only woke briefly at Ceylon, (now known as Sri Lanka) where two young ladies, wearing their lovely silk saris boarded the plane and handed us all a tin of Tea (Their country was, and still is, famous for its Tea) The boys went back to sleep after we had taken off again, but I, and still am the same, could not sleep a wink. Mike was fine. He did. But not me. Whenever I've made the trip back to the UK since (and I've don't that trip many times) I just can't sleep. I've tried sleeping tablets, but nothing works. But at least the boys and Mike were able to sleep for most of the long, arduous journey. I kind of knew that Australia was a long way away, but nothing could have prepared me for the distance. It took 27 hours of just sitting or lying on that plane. The break-up of the journey, landing at Ceylon, made the whole flight a little better, but still, it's not for the faint hearted.

By the time we had arrived at Kingsford Smith Airport in Sydney, I felt like a zombie. I was numb, dazed, sleep deprived and feeling like absolute shit. And my mind was also affected as well. What the heck had we done? Why had we come all the way to the other side of the world to live? What had possessed me? But I didn't have long to mull on this as we were shown through Customs (why did we have to go through such a scary procedure just to live in Australia, my young mind thought) Once we'd gone through Customs, and collected our three suitcases, we walked out into the

Arrival's Hall where a man, in full chauffeur's uniform, was holding up a sign with our surname on it. I asked him (stupidly) if he was waiting for us, and was told, yes, the government usually sent a bus to take migrants to the Hostel at Fairy Meadow in Wollongong, where we were bound, but as we were the very last of the 'Twenty Pound Poms' to arrive from the UK, they had sent, of all things, a white stretch limo and chauffeur for us. It was parked outside the airport entrance and I couldn't believe my eyes. If this was how Australia treated people, well, I knew I'd made the right decision to come here. (When I say 'I', I mean it quite literally. Mike did, and had always, gone along with whatever I had done and asked him to do. It wasn't that I was in any way 'bossy', (As I write this, I am thinking that I am coming across as really bossy to Mike. But it really wasn't like that. I seriously DID have to make all the decisions in our life. Mike just was never interested in doing anything and would never suggest anything. He also never murmured when I'd made what should have been a 'joint' decision. He just didn't care. it was just that he really didn't have any of his own thought processes at all.) In the stretch limo outside, I was amazed at how high and blue the sky was, at the way that every house was a 'bungalow' (single story house) and at how wide the roads were. It reminded me of American movies I had seen. The landscape and the vibe were the same. But as we drove to Fairy Meadow, I was wracked with anxiety. I only had $32 to my name, and how much was this limo going to cost me? The journey through outer Sydney

CRY

from the Airport, then onto the main road to Wollongong took just under an hour. The drive kindly stopped at a 'Look-out' place, which saw the whole of Wollongong stretched out before us, with the Ocean, my first sighting, in the background. But I was too worried about the money aspect of things to really appreciate it. Once we pulled into Fairy Meadow I needn't have worried, as when we reached Fair Meadow Hostel in Wollongong, a large City by the Ocean, on the south-east coast of Australia, the Chauffeur took our bags out of the boot, showed us where the Office was and wished us good luck. Embarrassed at not being able to 'tip' him, as I thought was expected of me, I could only tell him "Thank you". I noticed immediately We then made our way over to the Office and were told that rent was due on the first pay day after Mike started work. To my immense relief, we were told that we didn't have to pay anything yet We were given four of everything: cups, glasses, plates, cutlery etc, two blankets and a pillow each, and to my amusement, ONE skinny toilet roll, and then the key to our Nissin Hut, a cream, round, tin hut, Number 15. The huts themselves were set in rows. There was one toilet block between four huts, and a large canteen, which served us three meals a day. The day we arrived (12th June 1973) those wonderful, blue, sunny skies we'd seen at the Australian Expo in Manchester now gave us a sad welcome. It was pouring with rain. Now call me naïve, but I didn't think back then that it ever rained in Australia. But raining it was, so the first thing we did after making the beds up in the Hut, was to ask where the local shops were. We then walked, in the rain (we had brought no winter clothes whatsoever with us thinking we would never need them. Wasn't it sunny all year round in Australia? (Sure it is, NOT!) We got soaked to the skin, but somehow, it didn't matter. The sky, although not blue, certainly looked 'higher' and the smell, that smell of a different country that you can't quite describe, was intoxicating. We were actually IN Australia. It was hard to take in, having spent almost all of our lives in Birkenhead. We soon found the small row of shops in Fairy Meadow (just that name alone, made it all sound so exotic to a 'Girl from Birkenhead') We found a shop that sold raincoats, and with the last of our money, I bought two little yellow rain capes and matching sow wester hats for the boys. Mike and I had to do without, but we didn't care. We were in a completely different Universe to the one we'd just left yesterday.

We had arrived on a Tuesday, and on Thursday Mike started work at the Steel Works in Port Kembla, an Industrial suburb of Wollongong, along with many others from the Hostel, all recent arrivals, like ourselves, and who had been sponsored by them. There was a mixture of European cultures: Greeks, Italians and British, amongst others. The boys and I, over the six months we were to be living on the Hostel, immersed ourselves into Hostel life. Someone was always having a Tupperware Party, or afternoon tea, or for us Brits, just a 'cuppa' and a chat. Friendships were made (although not always kept up, as we all

CRY

eventually went our separate ways). However, the majority of people there were British like us, so we all felt connected to each other in some way. I did phone home a few times. My Mum, by now divorced, had got herself a house phone. Back then, in 1973, you had to go to the Post Office and book and pay for your three or six-minute call, then stand outside the phone box and wait for the operator to ring you at the pre-given time. When you only had ten seconds left, the operator would interrupt, telling you to end the call. My few calls to her consisted of me telling her what our new life was like, and she telling me any news about my three younger sisters, two of whom were still living at home with her. I can only remember missing my Mum once. I don't know what brought it on, but we were supposed to go to Minnamurra Falls (A local waterfall attraction) one Sunday with some friends, and without warning, I completely broke down, the first time I had ever done so. In retrospect, I suppose it was the anxiety of applying, then the waiting, to come to Australia, and the stressful life I had led, especially with Mike. However, I soon got over it. It wasn't as though I actually loved my Mum, was it?

On Boxing Day 1973, the Australian Government brought five hundred families from the Middle East to live on the Hostel. And from then on, life changed, as their culture was just so, so different from the Europeans. The women let their children go to the toilet in the sinks (even holding them over) instead of using he actual toilets, and the canteen become a different place altogether. Gone was the British fare that we were used to, the Fish and Chips every Friday, Cottage Pie, The Full English Breakfast etc. only to be replaced by what was, to us, 'foreign food'. A delegation was sent to Management, but nothing changed. The newly arrived men would go into the canteen first, eat their food, drink, then talk amongst each other, then the women would come in, clear their men's mess away and feed their children, then, finally, themselves. This was all very foreign to the rest of us there, and a large 'gap' came between the migrants. The newcomers would congregate in the public areas en masse, men in one area, women and children away from them, in another. They would almost bully the rest of us to go somewhere else if we dared to be in 'their space'. Frustrated, the majority of the British, Greeks and Italians, who had been on the Hostel for months, decided enough was enough, and moved off.

One evening, when we had only been at the Hostel for a week or two, we had a knock on the hut door. This was something that never happened. Nobody has ever knocked on our door that late in the day. I was almost too afraid to open it but Mike did, only to find a man offering to loan us the finance to buy a car. We found out he was a Finance Company Salesman and it was his job to get as many of us migrants to sign on the dotted line. As the majority of those on the Hostel worked at the Steelworks, the man knew that we would easily pass the credit check. Naturally, I bit his hand off. A car to go with our brand-new life! I couldn't

CRY

believe our luck. I gave no thought as to if we could afford it and the following day saw us driving back to the Hostel in a big green station wagon (I think they are called 'Estate' cars in the UK). We were also, like many others on the Hostel, scammed by a man selling blocks of land up in Queensland. The block was on an Island in the Great Barrier Reef and the pictures he showed us were stunning. A new car and a block of land up in the sunshine! Wow. We'd certainly hit the big time. However, all was not what it seemed. We paid that block of land off for three years, until a story in the Media alerted us to the fact that the land was un-useable, boggy, and with no services which could be installed there. Also, many others had also been sold the same block of land as us. The group of fraudsters were sent to jail, but that didn't help us, or all the people they had scammed. We lost thousands of dollars, as did others, although I was embarrassed that I had allowed myself to be scammed like this. The same thing, while we were still living at the Hostel, also happened with an Encyclopedia salesman. Well into the evening, we were talked into buying, on Hire Purchase of course, a set of Britannica Encyclopedias. We never paid fully for them, stopping the repayments after about nine months. But for some reason, we did get one letter, which we ignored, but then heard nothing else from the Finance Company. Maybe they'd gone bust? Who knows? We moved a few times over the next five years. We bought bits and pieces for the house and the children whenever Mike got paid. In 1974, don't ask he me how, but we had another son,

Leo. I had desperately wanted a girl, but Leo was the light of my life, and two years later, again, I've no memory of how, but we finally got our daughter, Shelby. When I say I have no memory of how, I can really only guess, as all as my four children were conceived virtually by my own hand. Mike had to be 'persuaded' and at that age, I wasn't very successful, or persuasive to a great extent, but I must have done something right to get four children out of a man who was devoid of any sexual feelings. I was determined to make it a happy family, unlike my own childhood, and did whatever I could to keep the children happy and content. They all played sports and went to private schools. But me? I was as unhappier than ever. Mike and I had been married for eight years when I had Samantha. I had gotten into the habit, about once every month or two, of 'persuading' him to have sex, not because I wanted it, but I needed his love, his affection and his attentions. Why, I couldn't tell you, why flog a dead horse? But that's what I did, year in, year out. Of course, I planned on numerous occasions to leave him and just take the children and start up on my own, but somehow, I just never seemed to have the guts. I had no confidence back then in my ability to actually live on my own, and bring up the children, although that is essentially what I was doing with Mike. I am quite confused about why I never went and got a job (in fact I never started work until we'd moved to Canberra and Shelby as nearly six) but stayed at home. I suppose I wanted to be a 'Home Maker' for the children. I cleaned and I cooked, took them to

CRY

Scouts, sports, etc. In 1976, we got a Housing Commission (Council) house. It had four bedrooms and a good-sized garden. We put an above ground swimming pool in and we seemed set for life. The boys went to the school over the road, and once a fortnight, on pay day, we would go to a Café and have something to eat, leaving us short, as always on money for the rest of the period. The year before I had gone with my friend, Anne, to a new Squash and Racquetball Courts which had opened. We played Racquetball (The ball is much larger than a squash ball, as is the racquet) and the owner suggested we try a squash ball and racket. Anne found this much too hard, but I, for some reason, took to it like a duck to water. At the time, the Ladies Competition, which plated every Tuesday evening, had 14 Divisions. That's where I started. Within a year, I was playing A-Grade Squash. I became obsessed. I think it took my mind off things and I found that was super competitive. Most weeks I would play seven to ten times a week. There was a Club nearby, which had two Squash Courts upstairs, and sometimes, after going to bed, around 10pm, I would get up, get dressed, and go to the Club and see if there was anyone playing. There would usually be a couple of men there, and I would join in for a game. Because of this, I was renowned for hitting the ball hard, much harder than the other girls. I embarrassingly developed into a bit of a 'John McEnroe' and at one stage, became quite intimidating (was this my ager from my past life coming out? Maybe.) On my way up to Division 1, I went for two years without losing. I had to have a three month break to get over being beaten (I know! Ridicules brat that I was!) but then went back and started coaching the Juniors, before starting Competition up again, this time being humble if I lost. Then out of the blue, Mike lost his job at the Steelworks, so we had to apply for benefits. These were paid by cheque from Social Security, and would come in the post, every second Friday. Naturally, by that day, we didn't have a cent to our name and would eagerly await the mail man on his motorbike. However, there were quite a few times when the mail man would drive straight past us, making my stomach sink. We would have to get the kids ready and walk the long way down to Wollongong town center to the Social Security Office, where they would promise to send another cheque out on Monday. They then told us to go to an Australian charity, St. Vincent de Paul, who would give us vouchers for our local supermarket. The only exemptions on these vouchers was that you couldn't buy pet food or cigarettes. So our poor dog had to have the scraps from our food, and Mike would have to go without his smokes. (Didn't make much difference as he was a miserable bugger anyway and would go around the streets collecting 'dog-ends' to make into a ciggie!)

Now it may seem as though life for me had somewhat settled down into family life, and in a lot of ways it had. I had my adored children, who gave me as much love as only your children can, and I was

CRY

determined to be the mother that my own mother hadn't been. Even though we were still quite poor, especially after Mike lost his job, we still went every Sunday (when it wasn't raining) to the Trash and Treasure, a flea market down in Wollongong center. Each week, I would send Ian away to walk around with the children, so they wouldn't see what I was buying (I'm a big believer in surprises! I hate knowing what's in a parcel.) and I would buy whatever toys I could afford without them seeing, so that Birthdays and Christmases were always filled with lots of presents, often, too many. But that's how I coped with being a Mum. I took the boys to Cubs, and then Scouts, paid for them to go on Camps and Excursions, they all had the correct uniform. The same at school. I'd like to think that they would have been the smartest and best dressed kids in the school. But what about my own wellbeing? While I was able to get some much-needed love and admiration from my children, from Mike, well, why would he have changed? Of course, he wouldn't, not by now after being married for so long. Over the years, I've always wondered just WHY he stayed with us. What was it that he actually got from having a wife and four lovely children? He barely interacted with them, and well, you know exactly what he got out of me. So why stay? I've never thought to ask him. I've always been too focused on why I never left him until we'd been married for fifty years. I've no intention of asking him now as I no longer speak to him, but it's something I'd love to know. Neither I nor the children would get barely a word out of him and even though he was not violent, as my Mum and Dad had been with me, he had little, or no, connection with them. As for our time in bed, well, we may as well have had separate rooms. Many years later, I was to get a Diploma in Mental Health from College, so I now understand that the love of your children, especially with a background such as mine, is never enough. That closeness, the intimacy, the holding, the tenderness, the kind, loving words, it's what most women need, and boy did I need it. It was easy to see that by now, I became depressed, and started on what was to be lifelong medication. I put all of my unrequited love into my Squash, being both competitive and obsessed. I played for Dapto Squash Club for ten years, rising to A-Grade level, and Coaching the youngsters. Stuart started High School, and the others were all in Primary School. And I was in exactly the same situation that I had been in since I was sixteen! Alone.

One day, as I walked back home from Squash, I had a sudden realization. Mike had been out of work for two years by this time, and I thought "I don't want my children growing up like this". Mike had spoken (Yes, he did occasionally!) of joining the Royal Australian Air Force (RAAF) so when I got home I told him to go and fill in the paperwork at the Defence Force Recruiting Office in Wollongong. He must have had something that they saw in him that I hadn't, because six weeks later, he was in. His job, after Basic Training, was to input data into a computer, and after the twelve-week

CRY

Basic Training, which was hundreds of miles away in Elizabeth, which is in South Australia, he was posted to Canberra, our Capital City, which was around three hours away from Wollongong. The night he left was a very emotional one. As he had to be at the train station just before 6am the next morning, I had come to bed early, in the hope of a little bit of intimacy before he left us for three months. I needn't have bothered. By 1.0am, he was still in the living room watching TV. By this time, I was incandescent with rage. His last night and he couldn't even give his wife of 12 years a little bit of intimacy. I started a huge argument, and all of my pent-up frustrations and emotions came out. Even though I told him what a shit husband he had been to me over the years, how he had ignored me, not talked to me properly, had no emotional or physical connection with me, that I may as well have been a single mother, I can't remember what else I said, but, as usual, what do you think he did? He said nothing. Just got into bed and was about to go to sleep. This increased my frustration and, of course, anger, even more. I told him I never wanted to see him again, and not to come back, I hated his guts etc etc. You get the picture! At that time, I had had enough. My crying and the argument (although one-sided) went on for what was left of the night, and at 5.50am, I drove him, still crying, to Wollongong Station, where he was to get a train to Sydney, where he would be sworn into the RAAF, and then transported to Elizabeth in South Australia, thousands of miles away, to do his Basic Training. But then, after he'd gone, something quite strange happened. I cried for him every day for a fortnight. I carried on playing squash, but could barely eat and my once well-rounded body became lean. For the first time since a child, I was actually thin. I wrote to him, on PINK paper and envelopes, every single day for three months. I gave him all the news of the day, what the kids had done, how my Squash had gone. Why, I have no idea. Ok. So by now, some of you may be saying "Arrh. Maybe she really did love him". But did I? I really don't think so. I think that this would be the FIRST time I was left on my own, and maybe, I really don't know for sure, but just maybe, I didn't think I could cope on my own. It's the $50,000 question! On Mike's first home leave, about two months later, it was the only time in our married life that I respected him. He stood resplendent in his full RAAF dress uniform. He'd had his hair cut very short and looked much older than his 31 years. But his personality, or should I say lack of it, was no different. Even on his first night home on leave, he chose to 'enjoy' his return, in the bathroom, instead of in bed with me. Nothing new there.

With his Basic Training over, Mike was Posted to Canberra, Australia's National Capital. We rented a house, mostly paid for by the RAAF and were able to buy a more reliable car as his wage, plus the fact that he was in the RAAF, made it so much easier for us to get Credit. The 'Squash Culture' in Canberra was not as big as it had been in Wollongong, and, although I joined a local Club, it soon petered out. Now was the time when I decided to do something with my life. I decided I would become a Nurse. I fancied the idea of sitting on the edge of a hospital bed, chatting to the patients, maybe doing their hair or their nails. Sure! I went for the interview and nearly heaved when I was told what my duties as an Enrolled Nurse (you had to go to college to become a Registered Nurse) would be. But amazingly a few days later, I received a letter from Canberra Hospital telling me I had got the job. I wasn't sure I wanted it now though. Me? Wiping backsides? I didn't think so. That day, in our daily paper, The Canberra Times, there was an ad for Mature Aged Students to study at the Australian National University in Canberra (the ANU). There was to be a day where applicants would do a morning answering multiple choice questions, and the afternoon to write an essay of your choice. I got my first job as a Property Manager in a high-class suburb, where everyone, including my workmates, wore good quality clothing, something very new to me. I'd always been a bit of a 'blagger' (I'd had to be, married to a man who barely spoke a word!) and got the job for my personality, not for any experience (of which I had none). It was hard, I won't deny it. Over 200 rental properties to look after, and with no experience whatsoever, I found it stressful and extremely hard work for about the first six months. But I soon picked it up and found that I had 'gut instinct' when it came to knowing what tenant to place in a property. As my children grew, and all were at school, the pace was fast. Dropping them off, doing a full day's work, then picking them up from After-School care, then home to start dinner. I suppose this time in my life, with work taking the place of Squash, was taken up with day-to-day living. I never had time to think about why Mike was like he was. Why he used pornography (I was later to find out that his mentally retarded cousin had taught him how to masturbate to pornography when Mike was twelve, although I still can't understand why a boy, even one as young as twelve, would have to be 'taught'. I always thought that it came naturally, but that's Mike's explanation, and he's sticking to it!) Occasionally, when I could be bothered (I still had no wanting for sex, but would have liked some kind of intimacy) I would 'make a move' on him, and sometimes it worked, other times, it didn't. When it did work, though, it would be over in minutes. I'm sure now, that throughout our married life, Mike got no pleasure out of me. As for me, well, I'd had my share of boys and men drooling over me years ago. One thing I now don't understand: Why Mike and I never sat down and talked. Really talked, about his lack of interest in me, or the children for that matter, and his love of pornography. Again, another of life's mysteries.

Mike did nine years in the RAAF. With the prospect of him being Posted out of Canberra, where we were all quite settled, he decided not to sign up again, and left. While he was in the RAAF, he had trained in IT, Computer technology and he soon got a job doing this. However, with Stuart and Mark now having left home, Mike and I started reading Country Life, an English

CRY

Magazine, that showed the Country in all its glorious splendor. I can't remember which of us suggested it, but we decided to go back and live in England. A friend of mine suggested going to York, so, along with Leo and Shelby, who were 14 and 16 and still at school at that time, we packed up, sold what we weren't taking and flew back home. We'd been in Australia for 17 years and had taken out Australian Citizenship, so we held dual passports. This was also the year my Dad died. He and Mum had been divorced for quite a while, and Mum had got herself a new man, but Dad had remained on his own until he emigrated over to Australia. He had become involved with a 'New Religion' woman and had firstly moved in with her, then married her. But it never worked out. They fought dreadfully over my Dad's Catholic religion and his wife's 'New Age' one. At least once a fortnight, my Dad would ring me, sometimes crying, asking me to "go and get him" as he'd had a row with her. In some respects, during those five years, he had become like a child to me, which is remarkable in itself, owing to the childhood he had put me through. I always felt that I had to somehow 'care' for him, and to look after him, as he was rarely happy. He'd had a bad heart for a number of years, and, even though he knew we'd already made arrangements to move back to live in England, it's possible that Dad just 'gave up', knowing that I wouldn't be there for him anymore. It's just a thought, but who knows. We buried Dad in June 1990 and packed up and moved back to England in the

November. What followed was to make my life bearable, for a while anyway!

We were planning on giving Surrey in England a try, as we'd mostly only lived up North. But a chance conversation with a woman in the Passport Office in Canberra, told us that York was a lovely place to live, so that's where we headed. We sold most of our possessions and shipped over some treasured items (as well as Mike's computer, (and what was one it, of course!) and flew over in late November 1990. Of course, it was a huge novelty at first. There's no place like England close to Christmas. All the shops were decorated, Carols playing in every store and lights on everywhere. It went dark at 3pm every day, the sky was lower (and greyer!) than in Australia, but we loved it, as did our two youngest children, who'd come with us. (The older two boys had left home, had jobs and girlfriends so had stayed in Australia, promising to come over and visit us the following year.) We rented a cottage on a large block of land that included a woodland and a 'big' house. But boy was it cold. It was called the quintessentially English name 'Rose Cottage' Although it was rustic and full of olde worlde charm (right up my street!) there was only ONE portable heater in the whole property and Mike would hike it up and down the stairs when needed. The woman in the 'big' house told us to "get out and walk" but we were so cold we could barely move. We'd just left the Australian summer and 40 degree temperatures, and I just don't think she understood

CRY

why we couldn't go out walking. So, again, we have no option but to look for something more suitable, and move we had to. This time, we found a three bedroom more modern semi-detached house about half an hour out of York center, and with central heating, to rent. It was at this house, not long after we'd moved in, that Shelby, my daughter, who had her friend with her, came home from school and caught Mike watching Porn, (It was girl Lesbianism, naked, Porn involving gay sex) and it is a memory that has stayed with her all her life. (More on that later). Mike, having been in the RAAF in Australia, got a job easily enough in the Stores at the Air Force Base nearby and I very quickly got a job at the Nursing Home just around the corner. My job, completely alone on the shift, was to bath three residents every night (there were about twelve or so residents living there, most of them with dementia) and to make them their evening cocoa, and then put them to bed, before the night nurse came on duty. Now, I'd never done this kind of work before, but quite liked working with the oldies, and there was an electric chair contraption that fitted onto the edge of the bath so that the resident could sit in the chair, and then it turned around and lowered them into the water, where I would help them wash, then at the flick of a switch, the chair would lift them out of the bath, turn around and allow them to either stand up to be dried, or sat in a wheelchair, depending on their mobility. As for 'washing them', you've got to be joking!! Wash then down 'THERE'?? No way. I'm afraid I shirked my full duties when it came to bathing naked old folk, and yes,

I really am now sorry. I wouldn't like to be treated like that if I ever find myself in a Nursing Home. Once dried, I would have to dress them and put them to bed. Only problem with bathing them was the chair was so heavy I couldn't lift it. So I would ring Mike, who was two minutes away, and he would come and set the bath chair up for me, then come back later and take it down again and put it back in the cupboard. I lasted two weeks in that job. Hated it with a passion. Just as Nurses and Doctors are 'cut out' for the job, so must you be to care for the elderly. Unfortunately, I'm not and can only regret not washing them properly. However, to my credit, I can say that all of the other care I did give them in those two short weeks I worked there, was given with love and affection. They really were a lovely bunch of people whose lives were, sadly, almost at an end.

My next job was at a local, but large, Newspaper, in York. I was taken on as a Sales Rep and spent the first two weeks being trained. On my first day 'on the job' I was given an area of a large desk to work on. I was to ring up Businesses and talk them into my going out to see them and selling them advertising in the paper. Easy peasy! I can do that. But I never got the chance to. I'd only been at my new chair (there was a long table down the middle of a large room, where all the Sales Reps sat, with a Supervisor at the top end) for ten minutes, when Shelby's school rang me on the work phone (no mobiles in those days, and I had given my work number to her school as the emergency

CRY

contact) telling me that Shelby had not turned up at school, but a couple of the other students had told the teacher that Shelby and her friend Maria, were planning on running away. As I hung up from the phone call, and undecided on what to do, the Supervisor came to me and told me to follow her to the Office. Here I was told that 'personal phone calls' weren't allowed, and that this was to be my 'one and only' warning! So what do you reckon I did? Hang my head and meekly apologise? Tell the Boss it would never happen again? Wrong! I told them to "Stick yer Job up yer Arse" (Or words to that effect!!) and walked out. To mutterings and stares of all the other Sales Reps, I gathered up my coat and bag, and stormed out. Another job bites the dust. But, all was not lost, as in York, there was also a 'Free' paper, The Advertiser. As it's office was only a five minute walk from the newspaper I'd just left, I decided to go job hunting there. Naturally, being Australian (the Brits do love us Aussies I've found) and having such a good Sales Record with Yellow Pages the year before, I was immediately offered a job. I was to sell the 'Situations Vacant' page. I started the following day at an annual salary I could have earned in a month back in Australia, and made my short time there a huge success. Not only did I reach my targets every week, I often doubled them, and more. Now it might sound (well it does to me writing this) as though I'm 'bragging' slightly. But seriously, I'm just telling it as it was. I am a good salesman and can sell 'Ice to Eskimos', something, I suppose, comes from having to do all the talking in a marriage where only one of the couple does the talking. That's my take on it, anyway. So I'm doing well at The Advertiser, making a few friends, and earning my pittance of a wage, but after a month, well, as usual I'm bored out of my brain. One morning, a man rang me, and asked to put an Ad in the paper. It was for a Sales Rep for an up-market Magazine, Yorkshire Life. The company produced quite a number of 'Life' magazines around England and the clientele were all wealthy. Now this was my sort of thing. Instead of taking his Ad to put in our Situations Vacant page, I asked for his fax number. Why I had a copy of my Resume in my bag I have no idea, but I did have, so I gave the man, John, my background and sales success, and asked him if I could fax the Resume to him. He rang me back five minutes later asking me to go to Batley, an historic market town in West Yorkshire, the following day for an interview. I knew then that another job had bitten the dust.

At home, life as we know it went on. And on. Shelby did 'run away' not so much from Mike and I, but because she was a teenager going through what teenagers go through. But she came home. Mike and I trod on eggshells with her for ages, for fear she might run off again. She had to change schools. Or should I say, she was "asked" to change schools. Our youngest son had started at the local Comprehensive school, but, coming out of a Private Catholic school in Australia, hated it immediately, and to our amazement, we were told that he was at least a year behind the

CRY

English school curriculum. He was advised to get a job and return the following year and repeat. While he did get a part-time job at Asda collecting trolleys, he knew he was better than this, and applied to Birmingham University to do Art (his teacher at school had told us he had talent). He sent some samples of his work with his application, and was accepted. But because we hadn't lived in England for the minimum three years, we had to pay ten thousand pounds. So that's what we did. We took out a Bank Loan, not having anything like that amount of savings, and away he went to Birmingham. (He was into his second year there when he was mugged, and had his wallet taken. That was enough to send him scurrying back home and the ten thousand pounds was wasted). Shelby never finished her new school either. She was always fighting with one girl or another and she was also "asked to leave". Being almost fifteen, and it only being weeks away from the end of term, the Education Department refused to find her another school, so she got a job in York as a waitress, and, like her mother, didn't like that one, so got another in a Nursing Home, only to not like that one either, so got a job looking after greyhounds in a Commercial Stables. Anyone see a familiar pattern forming here? But you would be wrong, as only a month or so into that job, which she WAS enjoying, she went out on her moped (small motor bike) one lunchtime to get a sausage roll and was hit, head on, by a woman pulling out, on the wrong side of the street, in a white van. Shelby was thrown from her moped into the road. It was said her screams could be head a mile away! Poor Shelby ended up with a broken femur, and a shattered tibia and fibula. She endured eight hours of surgery to fix everything up and was in bed for months, on crutches and a wheelchair for two years. She got $32,000 compensation and lost two years off her teenage life.

I went down to Batley on the train for the Yorkshire Life interview and was offered the job on the spot. The highlight for me though, was that I got a company car. It was parked outside the office and John told me I could take it home there and then, and start the following day. (That seems to have been a constant with me. I always seem to be able to start the following day!) Yorkshire Life magazine showcased the best that Yorkshire, the County, had to offer. I was to be the 'North' Yorkshire Sales Rep, and best of all, I got to work from home. They paid my 'phone bill and some of my electricity. Naturally, being a sales job, we had Targets to reach each month, and I will admit that it was hard work. Once a month, I had to travel to Batley, where along with the other County Sales Reps, we would have a meeting (Can't remember what about!) then drive all the way back home again. What we were all after was a 'Full Page' Ad, with the back page being the most prized possession. Towards the end of each month, we Reps would be almost giving magazine space away, just to a) fill that Edition, and b) to hit our targets. One day, I noticed a gap in my market. Nobody was doing Hotel and Restaurant Reviews, unlike other Yorkshire Counties, so I asked if

CRY

I could do it. The idea was that if a Hotel or posh Restaurant paid for four Ads in the magazine that year, they got a full-page Review free. And so I became a writer for the first time. After getting agreement from an upmarket Hotel or Restaurant, Mike and I would go and have a three-course meal, have a chat to the Chef afterwards, then stay the night in their best room, if it was a Hotel (we were treated like Royalty, so prestigious was Yorkshire Life Magazine). Back at home I would then write around 1500 words on how wonderful the place was. But there's only so many times you can write good things about a meal, or a Hotel room, and soon, Mike was saying "Do we have to go?". I started writing short pieces for the magazine on market towns and tourist spots and they would appear in the magazine. I would be thrilled to see my name in print. Once I went down to London to interview Michael Palin (one of the Monty Python team) who had just returned from doing his TV Show 'Around the World in 80 Days'. He was just so lovely and well-liked by everyone and I even got a kiss from him. I also had a two-hour phone call with Mick from the Group ELO. He is the violinist in the Group and hails from Yorkshire, so I was planning on writing a celebrity piece on him. Mick and I got on so well together, even though it was over the phone, that I think if things had of been different, we could have ended up together. ELO had played a concert the night before I rang him (I had been there as I'd got free tickets) and Mick had said "Why didn't you come backstage after the Show and meet the boys?". Oh heck. Why hadn't I rang him the day before! To meet Mick, along with Jeff Lynn, well, I can only cry at missing out on that, can't I? Mick was about to go to Europe on Tour with ELO and took my number and said he'd ring me from there when he got the chance, and we would meet up when the band got home. But, as usual, I was getting bored. Was another job about to bite the dust?

I was never to meet up, or even hear from Mick again, but ELO remain one of my favorite Groups to this day. Before he had had the chance to ring me from Europe, one day, sat in my dining room/office, working on the latest edition of Yorkshire Life, it was the final day before cut-off, and I was desperately trying to reach my target. So I went through my box of cards with 'leads' on them. I stumbled across one for a Wedding Reception Venue that I hadn't previously contacted and, as we had a 'Wedding' Feature in that edition, I rang to see if I could get an Ad out of them. The girl who answered the phone, let's call her 'Lyn' told me that she was leaving due to illness. I asked her what her role was and she told me that she was a Personal Assistant to an aristocratic Baronet. She also looked after the Wedding Reception Venue's bookings, staffing etc. I could do that, thinks the ever confident me! I asked her how I could contact her employer, let's call him 'Sir James'. I was given his direct number and immediately rang it. Yes, he said, his PA had resigned and yes, he would be looking for another to replace her. He sounded very 'posh'

CRY

indeed, but as you can now imagine, small matters like that faze me not one iota. He took my number and said he'd be in touch. That Thursday, at 10pm, when Mike and I were in bed making mad passionate love (did you just believe that bit??) the phone went. It was Sir James' wife, we will call her 'Lady James' for convenience, (even though it's quite a ridicules name for an aristocrat's wife!) and she, in a 'plum-in-the-mouth- voice, asked me if I could go to their house (A large Georgian Mansion with outbuildings and cottages) that Sunday at 10am. Is the Pope a Catholic? Of course I could (said with equal posh tones, I might add!). I was told that I must be discreet, as another member of their staff had applied for the position when 'Lyn' had left. Now, 'Sir James' didn't think that this girl was up to the task (and by heavens, was I to find out just how hard those tasks were to be!) but he had to, as a moral obligation, 'give her a go'. But he was quite convinced that she wouldn't work out, So Sunday morning saw me in my best bib and tucker sitting in 'The Library' (his office) in an antique easy chair, opposite 'Sir James, and being quizzed from a sheet of paper, which I later found out a lot of aristocrats use when hiring staff. I was asked questions like "If I were to ask your friends what you were like, what would they say?", all stupid questions like that. After about an hour of this, 'Sir James' asked me to come back the following Saturday to do a typing test, as that was what the majority of the job was about. On Monday, I went for the Yorkshire Lie meeting, and my heart just wasn't in it. As far as I was concerned, I'd got another job, a 'dream' job, actually, as I had often imagined myself as a PA (even though I'd never been one!) to either a Writer or a wealthy man with a Library. So here was my 'dream' come true. I felt that the upcoming typing test would just be a formality. I wasn't a good typist (although I've got a lot better over the years) but my usual confidence (where did I get it from??) let me believe I'd pass the test with flying colors. It was a long week while I waited for Saturday to come around, but suddenly there I was, in the 'Big House', in what was to become my office, faced with using either an electric typewriter or, something I'd never used before, a computer. The Estate Manager met me and showed me into the office and gave me a small Dictaphone tape with a long missive on it. Heck!! He asked me if I'd rather use the typewriter or the computer. Not knowing how to even turn it on, I chose the typewriter. I out the tape into the player and 'Sir James' voice came out. I was to write the following letter to the Archbishop of so and so, and "using the Debrett's Peerage and the Oxford English Dictionary, address him correctly." Wow. Even for the super-confident me, this was a step too far. I was able to find out how I would address the Archbishop, but the wording of the letter used was way beyond any words I have ever used. And if I'm honest, they were quite rude, talking about 'Homosexuals'. Naturally, I kept making mistakes, and frustratingly had to keep trying and starting over again. The Estate Manager came in a few times to see if I'd finished, then 'Sir James' himself, in a long pink dressing gown, entered the office. But somehow, I have no idea how, I managed to finish it just as he came in. He read it over and said "You're not very good at apostrophes, are you?", and that was it. He said he'd "be in touch" and away I went, quite deflated, certain that my lack of punctuation had been my downfall. Back at Yorkshire Life, I worked half-heartedly. My 'dream job' had escaped me, and for once, I had no idea what to do next. About six weeks later, with 'Sir James' forgotten, I received a 'phone call from the man himself. Would I like to start next Monday? Would I what!!!

THE COTTAGE BY THE BECK

The job with 'Sir James' came with a small, but absolutely beautiful, two-bedroom cottage. It had a long, lovely garden, which led down to a gently flowing, narrow beck (like a stream). Mike and I still had Shelby and our youngest son, Terry, living with us. Luckily there were two living rooms downstairs and two bedrooms upstairs, so Leo used the second living room as his bedroom. The kitchen was so tiny that only one person at a time could be in it, but with a window seat, where we would sit and watch the multitude of birds through a set of small binoculars, and a row of mature rose bushes outside that window, it was heaven. It was only a short walk to work for me, although a longer drive to the Air Force Base for Mike. I was paid quite well for the time, twelve thousand pounds a year, and when 'Sir and Lady James' were down in London (Sir James worked and had a house there) myself, the 'Houseman' and the Housekeeper/Cook, would use the great Georgian Mansion like our own, sitting in the lovely rooms drinking tea and chatting. 'Sir and Lady James' would have had a fit if they'd have known. Every morning, before he left for London, 'Sir James' would leave on my office floor, a number of piles of files to be worked on. Each pile had a different colored Post-it note stuck to the top file: Red being urgent, then blue, then yellow etc. As I'd usually have a week to finish all this work and he was back from London, it was an easy job. I can even remember my very first note that I had to type (the girl who had been given, then refused, the try-out of the job before I had started, had spent an hour with me on my first day, showing me the ropes, and especially, the computer, so I became quite efficient at it.)It was 'Sir James' saying (for me to type and do three copies: one for him, one for his wife, and

CRY

the third for my files) "Trish, a note to my wife in these terms. Darling, please do not, Trish underline not, buy that disgusting Earl Grey tea from Fortnum's. I despise it. Trish, sign all of my notes to my wife with an 'R'". The extent of the work was notes to his long-suffering wife, and letters to the newspapers on matters he had his own high-handed opinion on, to the Parish Council, on which he sat, The Village Hall Committee, and to villagers, living mostly in cottages he owned. There were sometimes notes to myself if someone had offended him in any way. What he expected me to do about it I have no idea! The subject matter was as strange as it was varied and one thing I can say is that I was never bored.

One day, the couple held a dinner party for the glitterati of the County (other aristocrats like themselves) and around 4pm, 'Lady James' rang me from her 'Boudoir' (office) next door to me, and asked if the gamekeeper had brought the six pheasants in as she'd ordered earlier, as they needed plucking and cooking ('Sir James' would never have salt used, or any kind of flavoring at all. Just either game birds or rabbits from The Estate and vegetables from the walled garden, all just boiled in water) and time was getting on. When I rang the Gamekeeper, a curmudgeonly old grump, who had been working on the Estate for many years, he told me in no uncertain terms where to tell 'Lady J' to go. She had never ordered any birds from him, he said. She's losing her marbles!! When I told Lady J this, she was quite annoyed, sure that she had asked for the six birds, then told me to ring the man back and get him to shoot six pigeons. That would have to do. (On these aristocratic Estates, the Gamekeepers are often treated like Gods, especially if they have been there for many years!). As I was walking home that afternoon, I heard exactly SIX shots being fired, Dinner is served Ma'am.

The following morning, they had gone down to London, so we 'servants' had the house to ourselves. I went into the kitchen to see the dog's bowl overflowing with a grey meat. It was the pigeons from last night. Sue, the Housekeeper, told me that the meat on the pigeons was still full of 'shot' and all of the guests had sent it back. Hence the lucky old dog getting it. A few days later, the accolades started to arrive from 'The Hon' this and that, thanking Sir and Lady James "for such wonderful hospitality and, as usual, such a lovely meal". Seriously, until you've worked for the aristocracy, you have no idea of how they live their lives. The Wedding Reception Venue, for which I was also responsible, was a thorn in 'Sir James' side. He hated the invasion of his property (The venue ran almost parallel to the big house, and often, if we had a wedding on, guests would wander across to the big house and look in the windows). Many a time I've had an 'urgent' RANT tape from Sir J, saying that a wedding guest had looked into his dining room window and watched him and Lady J eating. On one occasion, the rant was particularly bad, as a car had been parked close to Sir James' own car. I was told to investigate who the owner of such madness could be, only to find out that it was the Lord Mayor's car, with the chauffeur sitting inside it for the duration of the wedding. Sir J didn't give a jot whose car it was. A letter was immediately dictated, telling the Mayor it was "not a bloody carpark (Trish underline 'not')" Our Houseman, Jack, a lovely man in his early 60s, whose job it was to fetch the wood and keep the fires going, as well as acting as chauffeur and general handyman, also looked after the practical side of running the Wedding Reception Venue, setting up the correct number of tables, ordering the booze etc. (We had an outside Caterer) But one day, Jack announced that he'd had enough. It was all getting a bit too much for him. He would stay on as Houseman, but wanted to give up the Weddings (which would usually go on until two or three in the morning from three or four the previous day) so I asked Mike, who, in a moment of excitement, had mentioned that he was getting fed up of all the travelling to and from the RAF Base, if he would like to take over the Weddings. I stupidly thought that maybe, just maybe, working together at close quarters, would bring us closer. Did it? What do you think? So for the next year or so, Mike would look after what Jack had previously done. His parents, having run a Pub, meant that Mike knew alcohol, how much to order, and what was popular. And so life went on. Shelby started work at a greyhound stables, mucking out, and generally looking after the racing dogs. She bought herself a little moped, a red and white Honda 50cc, which she whizzed around Malton and York on. One lunchtime while working at the kennels, Shelby decided to go out to the bakery on her Honda. On the way there, a woman, parked on the wrong side of the road, pulled out and hit Shelby head on. She was flung off the bike and into the road. I later found out her screams could be heard a mile away. I was at work in my office in the Big House at the time when a nurse from Scarborough Hospital rang to tell me there was nothing to worry about, but Shelby had come off her bike (I just thought she had slipped on the wet winter leaves!) but she then went on to tell me the extent of her injuries. She had completely broken in two her Femur, and shattered her Tib and Fib, the two bones that make up your leg below the knee. After two surgeries, months in bed, further months in plaster, external fixators and crutches, Shelby, after two years, could finally walk again. The woman who had caused the crash got off with a slap on the wrist and Shelby received $32,000 compensation.

Our youngest son, Leo, had also came back to live in England with us, but he was a petulant, moody and rude teenager. As he got a bit older, I would tell him, Leo, go back to Australia, travel around the world, do something but just go. His constant bad behavior and moaning was really getting on my nerves. While Mike never offered any support, there was one instance when I came home from work and found a dead pigeon in our tiny kitchen. Its head, dripping blood, was hanging over my sink. When I asked if he really

CRY

did have to put this kill in my kitchen (Both Mike and I had grown up City folk and had no affinity whatsoever with country life and living!) Leo gave me a mouthful (I can't remember what he said, but it was terribly rude and disrespectful, in line with the late teenage years he was going through). Mike, for the first time ever in his life, lifted Leo by the neck and put him up against the kitchen cupboard. "Don't you ever speak to your mother like that again"! Wow! Respect! I never knew he had it in him. Leo stormed out and I followed him, as he was saying that Mike had 'broken his jaw'. I persuaded him to come back home and then took him to the local cottage hospital, begging him to not say that Mike had done it. No idea why I was protecting him, but I saw a different side to Mike that day. Leo's jaw wasn't broken, just his wounded pride, but still he moaned and moaned about having to live 'in this shithole of a Country' (England). I got sick and tired of telling him that the world, at his age, now eighteen, was his oyster. He could work his way around, just as thousands of other youngsters do, but no, he never moved. Instead, on the advice of his school teacher, who saw some promise in him in his Art, he applied, and was accepted, into Birmingham University. He lived in digs, spent every penny of his quarterly Student Loan on rifles to shoot wildlife (where on earth did he get that from, I will never know! (If any of us saw an injured bird or pheasant on the roadside, he could calmly go over to it and break its neck, putting it out of its misery!) and other 'Countrified' things, then come begging me for money. He passed his first year

Ok. He even sold his first-year Collection to a Businessman from Scotland. However, not long into his second year, he was mugged in Birmingham and had his wallet stolen at knifepoint. That was it for Leo. This 'shit of a Country' just got even shittier and he came to live with Mike, Shelby and I after we had moved to Abingdon, in Oxfordshire.

In 1993, it was Mike and I's 25th Wedding Anniversary. Having no friends to invite to a Party, I thought it would be a good idea (and fulfil my need for excitement!) to go to Egypt, a place that had fascinated me for years. We left from York Station and made our way down to Heathrow. Seeing Mike's usual glum face, I asked him "What's up? Don't you want to go?" He replied "Don't care really"! That upset me all the way to Egypt, and I just couldn't get his comment out of my mind. I now thought that this holiday might not have been such a good idea after all! (More on this later.) However, it was while I was working for Sir James, I had developed Repetitive Strain Injury (RSI) in both arms (probably because of the mound of typing I'd had to do in the three years I worked for him!) In fairness, he did get a Temp in, but I was constantly having to check and change her work, so demanding was he, so that didn't last. I started typing with one hand, holding a pencil with a large square rubber on the taped to it, but nothing helped. They paid for me to have acupuncture, physiotherapy, and to see a Specialist, but in the end, I had no option but to give in my Notice, as typing was the mainstay of my work. Unfortunately, the lovely idyllic cottage by the beck

CRY

came with the job, so this meant that we had to move out. Leo was t University in Birmingham, and Shelby had moved in with a friend, so there was just Mike and I. It was during this time that I planned the first serious attempt at escaping. While I was working out my Notice, I bought a copy of 'The Lady' magazine. This weekly publication, which still publishes today, had quite a few pages every week of Domestic and the type of work I had been doing for Sir James, in it. I found a job that would have suited me down to the ground, a companion for an elderly lady, in a gorgeous thatched cottage. She wanted no housework done (that's just not me!) as there was a Housekeeper who also cooked. It was in Northamptonshire, 'Down South' as us 'Scousers' say. The following Saturday (I can't remember if I had told Mike I was going) I got the train down from York, then a taxi to the cottage. The ladies' name was Edith, and we hit it off straight away. After chatting with her for about two hours, she offered me the job on the spot. Only one problem. She was not offering a salary, just my food and board. I told her I'd think it over and let her know by the following morning, but on the train back to York, I'd already made my mind up. No salary was no good for me. I had no car, no savings and two children still living in the UK and two back in Australia, So back to Mike in Malton I went. The following week, my last with Sir James, I again bought a copy of 'The Lady' and there was a position in it for a Domestic Couple to run a large household. I can do that, I thought and rang the number in the Ad. The posh lady who answered immediately, said (over some electrical noise," Hang on, the Duke is just vacuuming"!! She then shouted to the Duke to turn the vacuum off. I couldn't believe it! A Duke of the Realm doing his own cleaning? My mind boggled. An Interview was arranged for the Friday and the address was a Stately Home about three-quarters of an hour outside of Birmingham, where Leo was at University. Upon our arrival, there were peacocks in the immaculate grounds and a Rolls Royce in the sweeping driveway. We were shown into the Duke and Duchess's Sitting Room and the Duke wore an apron (Seriously!) They were impressed that we had both worked for Sir James and that we had no children living with us. The job itself was to run the household and manage the staff. We would also be required to wait at table when they had large dinner parties or shoots. We were taken to the top of their beautiful house and shown the flat where we would live. It was spacious and well appointed, and looked out over the grounds. Again, we were offered the job on the spot. Could we start next week, we were asked? But there was one problem. To come and go in and out of the house, we had to actually walk through it, and up their own staircase, to get to our flat at the top. Our main problem was that we had a dog and a cat, and this situation was no good for them, so, unfortunately, we turned it down. A day or so later, after the disappointment, I realized that I am no Housekeeper, or waiter on tables, so really, we had had a narrow escape, as I can't imagine we'd have stayed in that job for very long.

CRY

Mike hadn't changed one iota in all the years I had known him, but for some obscure reason, I had to keep trying. I just had to keep asking him to show me the affection and caring that I craved. I got him to repeat, parrot-fashion, words of endearment, he would, even though I found it all really pathetic. But hey! Anything to me was better than the nothingness that was my life with him. I have continually asked myself why I didn't just bugger off and start a new life somewhere? I think that probably it was largely down to money, or should I say, a lack of it, although there definitely was an aspect of 'control' in the way Mike dealt with me. With my time with Sir James coming to an end, we applied for a job for both of us in Sutton Courtenay, near Abingdon in Oxfordshire. The couple were 'New Money', he having made a lot of money from selling his very successful business, and with it, they had bought a run-down, large mansion-like house, in seven acres of land. The property had old stables, a swimming pool, its own small 'pub' and a three-bedroom staff cottage, in which we were to live. Shelby came with us, but Leo decided to stay up North and worked as a Gamekeeper, rearing all the poor little birds so that some rich man could try and shoot it down dead! In the beginning there, I was to look after their two young girls when they were away at their new business. I had to take them to school, pick them up again, give them their tea, bath and get them ready for bed. Mike's role was to make a garden out of the existing wilderness, (He'd never gardened in his life, but he ended up making a pretty good job of it!) and looking after their half a dozen or so chickens. (One night he forgot to lock them away and a fox got in and killed the lot). But as time went on (We were there about a year) I was expected to do more and more around the house, which the couple were renovating around themselves, causing all sorts of problems with dirt and dust. I've said previously, I might be many thangs, but a cleaner I am not. So I'm sure it's not going to take you long to work out what happened next? Yep, we gave our Notice in. I'm pretty sure the couple were quite glad that I, if not Mike, was going, as I had been complaining for a number of weeks that I didn't agree to cleaning the house, especially one which was being virtually gutted around them, when we'd had the Interview. But 'New Money' like their own way, and if they wanted me to now become a cleaner, a cleaner I would become. But not me. I'm not made that way. Mike very quickly found a job in Bath with a Publishing Company. About six months earlier, our son, Mark, and IT wiz, had come over from Australia, and, with his IT background, had easily found the job at the Publishing Company in Bath. Hence, he was able to get Mike a job there (he had always been into Computers. In fact, that was his job in the RAAF.) Mike's job was to check all the Computer-related CD's which came free on the front of every Magazine each month. He would work ten days a month, and was paid the equivalent of a month's salary, on which we could just about live. We had managed to rent a beautiful old cottage, full of beams and charm, and was hundreds

CRY

of years old, in Dorset, which is in the South of England. Leo came with us, and Shelby, having recently broken up with her friend whom she had been living with, also rented a house a few miles away from us. She held down three part-time jobs, but all was not right for her. I, for the first time since Shelby had been five, decided not to go to work at all. Instead, I found a writing partner, a middle-aged woman, Val, who was a Talk-Show Host on the local Radio Station. We'd bumped into each other in Waitrose, our local supermarket, and had stood chatting near the meat aisle for over an hour, before deciding that she would visit me the following day. It wasn't long before we were collaborating on a Play for TV. We both got enormous pleasure out of writing simultaneously from our individual homes, and sending what we'd written back and forth between our houses. When we'd finished it, we sent the Play to Channel Four who, three months later, wrote back, saying it had promise, but we'd need to build the main characters up a bit more, then send it back into them. But before we could do so, Val's husband found her dead in bed one morning. She'd had a brain aneurysm and died instantly. It was the first time I had lost a friend and I had a knee-jerk reaction. We moved back to Australia. It wasn't just Val's death that brought this move on but a combination of things. Firstly, Mike lost his job in Bath. They had offered for him to become full-time, but He'd declined, so out the door he went. Then, in the same week, our car failed to pass its MOT as it was full of rust, and we didn't have the money for a new one, then the final straw (all of this happened in the same week!) we got a letter from the owners of the cottage giving us four weeks' Notice. They wanted it back so they could use it (and make more money, I'm sure!) as a Holiday Let. So I sold (once again) my collection of Agatha Christie books and my Royal Doulton and a few other bits and pieces, in order to get the air fare back. Leo had been working a fair way away as a Gamekeeper and didn't want to come back with us but Shelby did. We flew out of Heathrow Airport on 21st February 1998. We'd been back in England for over seven years. But what fantastic experiences I'd had, professionally!

Mine, and I'm sure most women's idea of a husband, is one of love and support maybe the odd gift as a show of affection, but most importantly, companionship and support. I was to get none of those from Mike whatsoever, for the whole 50 years of our marriage. Of course varying degrees of intimacy is expected, depending on the individual couple, but back then, still Mike remained silent and self-absorbed, regularly using pornography and masturbation, which I'm sure he was addicted to. But where did that leave me? I knew I didn't really want any physical relationship as I was still like a block of wood, with no 'feelings' whatsoever, but marriage is about SO much more than sex, Isn't it? But I had a plan brewing in the back of my mind. Once we were back in Australia, I intended to get a job, find a house (as a Property Manager that would have easy) then

CRY

take Shelby, and Leo if he changed his mind and came back, with me and leave Mike behind to love himself to his heart's content. As you know, by this stage, we only had Shelby and, possibly, Leo. Mark and Stuart had left home and were in their twenties. But Leo had decided to stay on in the UK (But was soon to return to Australia) so really, it was just Shelby and I. And if the boys wanted to come and stay, of course, they could. This time, I was quite determined that this was what I would do. Mike and I were finished (had we ever even started? I don't think so!) So I forged ahead, making secret preparations, although Mike wouldn't have neither noticed or cared, so there really was no need for any secrecy in planning my escape.

TRISH OLLMAN

ON THE ROAD AGAIN

Shelby, whilst still in her mid-teens, had developed what was thought to have been Munchausen's Disease. Around the age of fifteen, before she had had her Moped accident, she was going up to the hospital on a regular basis with unexplained stomach pains. Despite having many investigations over the course of about four years, nothing was ever found, and the Doctor mentioned Munchausen's. Around the time she was twenty, she was still going into hospital regularly, but this time, mental illness was thought to be the cause. I thought that by bringing her back with us to Australia, things might get better for her. But they didn't. Within a month of being back in Canberra, she was back in a Psychiatric hospital, where she was eventually diagnosed with Borderline Personality Disorder and, regardless of being prescribed numerous different medications, she never seemed to get any better. Over many years thereafter, she was to become a regular patient, going in and out of psychiatric wards on a regular basis. She did try and work, helping the disabled people pack knives and

CRY

forks etc into bags for Airlines, but that didn't last long. When we had arrived back in Australia, we had my son, Stuart's, Mother-in-Law's flat, which was under the main part of her house, to live in until we found a place of our own. I took a temporary job as a Receptionist at a Commercial Real Estate Agents, (I'd only ever worked in the Housing sector) but answering half a dozen phone calls a day didn't float my boat, so I went in search of a Property Manager's job, one which I had done for quite a while when we had last been in Canberra. Mike soon got an IT job with a Government Agency. As always, I was lucky enough to find another job straight away, again as a Property Manager, at which, by now, I was an old hand. I found the freedom of being able to just come and go as I pleased to be a huge perk, although I hated doing the routine inspections, and going into other people's homes, it seemed to me to be a huge intrusion. I also found that I had a real knack for putting 'good' tenants into vacant properties, for 'sussing' the good ones out of the often dozens of Applicants for a vacant property, so I rarely had any trouble with my tenants. But as my salary increased, so did my levels of boredom. I found that when I took on a new Property portfolio for a Real Estate Agent, the Rent Roll would often be in a bit of a mess, well, more often than not, a big mess. But within three months, tops, I would have no rent arrears, no vacant properties and everything running hunky dory. And so, as usual, I would easily get bored with nothing much to do, bored enough after no more than a year in any job, to start looking for something else. I was lucky that, in Canberra where I worked, I had gained a reputation amongst Estate Agents for being able to fix bad Rent Rolls, so I never had any trouble getting work. However, on the other side of the coin was Mike. I still hadn't left him. Why? I suppose it was just too easy to actually stay with him after all this time, sharing our salaries (two decent salaries I might add) pooling our salaries to pay the rent and groceries, electricity etc. I was still desperately unhappy underneath that 'strong, capable, persona, that lay dormant just beneath my skin, of course I was. He hadn't changed one bit. And after so long, I really didn't expect him to. But I think my work, and the accolades I received from my bosses, kept me going, for now at least, as I still planned to leave Mike 'soon', always 'soon'. But all the while, day in, day out, Mike was Mike. No change there, BUT they say 'Old Habits Die Hard'. One day, I came home from work at lunchtime to pick up something I'd left behind, and was surprised to see his car in the driveway. By now, we had been married for thirty years or so. Wondering why on earth he would be home at lunchtime, as he never usually was, I made my way to the Study, where I could hear him typing on the computer, and sure enough, there he was sitting working (doing goodness knows what!) on one computer. (Amazingly he had installed THREE without me knowing, although I must admit I did tend to leave him to himself back then, so the three computers might have been there for a while, for all I knew.) To my horror, on the other two screens were images of porn. I'll never forget the girl on the

CRY

screen closest to me. Aged about twenty, blonde, big bare boobs, and the part of her that definitely shouldn't have been on show, spread out with her hands, for all (or Mike!) to see. There was another porn picture on the middle screen which is too vile to write about. That he not only had it on there, but that it was there, in the background for him (as a 'comfort?') as he worked on something else, made me sick to the stomach. I walked over to him, slapped his face and told him to get out. As usual, he gathered up a few things then ended up sleeping in his office for two days, when, I wonder if you can guess what's coming? Yep, I let him back home again. And in only two days! In retrospect, I still feel that my reasoning for staying with Mike was always associated with money and his sly control issues. We often only ever had enough money to just get by, even with two reasonably good wages coming in, and I think that because we had married so young, and me straight out of an abusive family, maybe I was just too scared of being on my own. So far into writing this book, I can't help thinking that I should have called it 'WHY'? instead of 'CRY', because that's all I keep asking: WHY?

By now, Stuart had been married to a lovely girl, Paula, whose family had come from Chile. They bought a house and a good car, and after a few years of married life, Stuart decided to join the RAAF. He and Paula spent a long time with the Air Force in Queensland, where Stuart served as an Air Defence Operator. But after ten years, they decided to come back to Canberra and for Stuart to leave the RAAF. Soon after, and after the couple had been married for quite a while, my wonderfully talented grandson, Andrew, was born. I would have him every Monday, even teaching him basic reading until Stuart and Paula sent Andrew to a small boutique Private School, where he would spend most of his school life. But after ten years, Stuart's marriage disintegrated and they split up. Andrew would spend a week with his Mum and a week with Stuart. It seemed a reasonable arrangement, if not a little strained. Stuart re-married and went on to have a girl, my darling Angelina, and a boy, Lewis, two of the most beautiful, well-behaved children you'd ever find. They are all happy children, and Andrew has not long finished a double degree at University. He is destined for great things in the Computer Engineering field, and I couldn't be more proud of him. Mark had also married. A local girl who had known since school days. He had started out in Canberra's local newspaper's photographic dark room, but one day, there was a massive crash outside the newspaper's office, and there being no Photographers in the building, Mark grabbed a camera and ran outside and took pictures. They made the front page the next day, and his future career was set. He did teach himself the World Wide Web when it appeared in the 90's and was one of the first to use it professionally. He went on to become, the same as Stuart, a Webmaster and IT Professional. Both Stuart and Mark are wonderful and I am just so proud of how they've both turned out in the face of adversity. The

CRY

girl did good, hey! Leo, however, is a different story. After we had returned from England, (Remember, he had stayed on as a Gamekeeper in England, rearing young birds that one day would be shot down by the gentry who could afford to pay the landowners of Great Britain the exorbitant charges to fire a gun and try and shoot down some harmless bird for 'pleasure', and all in the name of sport! But he enjoyed it. After a year though, he decided to return to Australia. Now we don't have many Game Keeping jobs available (we don't shoot birds!) over here, so he went and worked on a farm in Victoria, fencing and welding, and helping with the livestock. I got on really well with him and we regularly kept in touch, even though he was a thousand miles away. He had a lovely girlfriend, Karen, but she wanted him to commit, and he didn't, so they parted ways. Shame really as I really did like her. But then he did a tour of Europe. He'd been working as a Monster Truck Driver in the coal mines up in North Queensland, and was earning the kind of money that he could certainly do things with. So, driving through Italy one day, near Como in the North, he came across 40 acres of land, a forest really, and a two-hundred-year old farm house for sale. However, it badly need restoring, but, seeing his dream of living off the land (He is a bit like Mike, quiet but thoughtful. So he bought it anyway, and came back to Australia to work and earn enough money in the mines to put a new roof on it. However, our dear friend Mr Covid 19 decided to come along about now, so Leo is stuck in Queensland, unable to get to the house in Italy, and has no idea when the world will open back up again. But that's not all. Just before Christmas 2019, I had my usual lovely phone call with my boy. We chatted about his roof in Italy and how much money he had saved, and of how he planned on going back to Italy when the European weather warmed up in the Spring, to finally get the new roof put on. But then on Christmas Day, when I tried to ring him, I just got his voice mail. I let a Christmassy message, asking him to ring me. But as January came and went, I realized (I was trying to finish Writing the Screenplay, 'Last Resort' to a deadline, one of my books, Escape to Paradise Island, which was being made into a Movie) that Leo hadn't rang since our pre-Christmas phone call, so very out of character for him, so very out of character for him. I tried every single day to contact him, without success, and even rang the coal mine where he had worked, only to be told he no longer worked there. I rang the local police in Mackay. No, they hadn't heard anything of him. So I put a Notice on the local Facebook Notice Board, with a photo of him. I got about fifty responses, some nice, telling me they had seen him at such and such a place, another saying she had just seen him in the local supermarket 'last week', but I was also to get the Trolls, as well. "Leave him alone. If he doesn't want to be found then just leave him." "He's a grown man. If he wants to be found, he will be. Leave him alone." But the most distressing of all was that I received a one line text from Leo himself saying "Take that down now!" Ok, well at least I knew he was alive, but what on earth was going on. We hadn't had a

CRY

single cross word and were a loving mother and son. Then, a man put on my Notice "I'm trying to hide him". What on earth did that mean? And that's were things stand today as I write. I have no idea where exactly he is, I haven't spoken to him since December, and it seems as though he might have got into some type of bother. I have tried to reach out to him, telling him it doesn't matter what he's done, to please, please get in touch and let me know he's alright, and if there's ANYTHING whatsoever I can do I will. But still not a word. Will I ever see my darling boy ever again? Who knows. And yet again, 'WHY'?

By this time, over the years, I had put on a heap of weight, and I was almost 130kgs, (all of my five siblings were to have the same life-long battle with weight! That has to say something about our early home lives, surely? A lack of any kind of treat - at least those which we hadn't stolen - and a diet of egg and chips (or similar, plus the emotional and physical abuse), I am sure has left all six of us deeply scared and problematic where food, and life are concerned! So even if I had wanted to find another man, I wouldn't have been able to get one. Who would have given ME a second glance? Not only did I hate myself for the way I looked, but also, believe it or not, for how Mike allowed me increasingly to speak to him, without retaliation, or even a word back, frustrated and angry at him as I had become. I'd held my emotions, and they were held extremely deeply, all of our married life, as well as bringing into our marriage my damage and need for love, which I had never had with either my family or with Mike. So me shouting and being angry at him was to become the norm in our house for the last few years of our 50 year marriage. And to this day, I am full of self-hatred of doing this, even though I know my actions were justified. Instead of letting things get to that stage, I should have 'ran for the hills' in 1967 when I had first spotted Mike at The Birkenhead Boys Club playing football. Or left in any one of the dozen attempts that I had to leave over the years. You try living for so long with someone who barely speaks and give you no support, emotionally, personally or intimately. In July 2015, I had a Gastric Bypass, which saw me lose 56 kilos. A few weeks before the surgery, I visited my GP and asked her if I could come of my Tourettes medication, Risperidone. This drug was known the keep weight on you, and getting weight loss surgery and staying on Risperidone didn't seem an option. My Doctor took me off it over two weeks (tapered, she said) However, on the day of my surgery, the surgeon asked me if I was chewing gum. Of course I wasn't, but I WAS sucking my mouth. Now, five years later, I now know that sucking to be called Tardive Dyskinesia. Instead of being taken off Risperidone over s six month period, and in consultation with a Neurologist, coming off it VERY slowly. I was taken off it over two weeks, and such drastic withdrawal caused this TD. I have tried every form of medication and pain relief there is to try, but nothing has ever worked. It drives me insane and is the bane of my life.

CRY

Over the years, Mike and I had just co-existed under the same roof for fifty years. That's it, and I became to bitterly resent him and what he was, of what he had made me become (a mere shell of my former self). But the older I became, and the longer we were married, the more like a 'nagging' wife, always trying to get Mike to change, I became. A few months before I left him, I had my boobs lifted and made smaller as I was like a prize cow just having been milked. I was thrilled with my new boobs. It was like I was 18 again. Mike? Didn't look at them. touch them, comment on them, nothing. Just as he had done with my massive weight loss. Which, if I'm honest, I'd had done both just for myself, certainly not in any way to 'Tempt" Mike (the only thing to 'tempt him, if I'm honest would be a room full of naked young prostitutes, splayed all over the floor, all for him to 'pleasure' himself with, although I doubt I could have afforded that. And just think, he could have had me with my new body and my new boobs, completely free!) I felt, although I still think I was justified, that now was to be MY time for a fresh start, given Mike's treatment of me, not only as a woman, but as a wife and, just as importantly, as a person, the mother of his children. I felt nothing for him by now and held no respect for him whatsoever. (Had I ever?) As he became older, he started to go deaf, so I naturally had to raise my voice just so he could hear me. Instead of ever giving me a response, he would just either shrug his shoulders, or roll his eyes, then turn and walk away. Have you got any idea just how frustrating that is, year in, year out? It's not very nice, let me tell you! Julia, who was living with us, saw my shouting (both angrily and not) at 'poor GP' (all the grandkids called him GP – Grandpa). The big bad wolf shouting at the quiet and wonderful Saint Mike. Friends and colleagues would say "Gee, Mike's pretty quiet, isn't he?" I, in turn, would be highly embarrassed, then, as the years went on, angry, and so the shouting continued.

Somehow, over the almost forty years of our marriage, we had never owned a house, always rented, so it was with some surprise that I suddenly found myself with six thousand dollars saved in the bank. That Plan I'd had before we left England, well this was it. Save enough money, spend little, and get a place of my own. Start again. But now that I did have that bit of money, two factors kept me from going ahead with my Plan. The first was my weight. I felt like an elephant. My self-confidence was non-existent. Even though Mike may have been emotionally and verbally bereft, at least he was SOMEONE. Suddenly, the thought of going it alone, even though I now know it would have been the best thing I could have done, didn't seem like a good idea. The second obstacle was Shelby. She needed stability, and even though Mike was never a 'proper' father to her, (he ignored her as well as me) he was still around, and again, I didn't feel confident that I could pull of my Plan. So we did what everyone in our situation does in times of crisis: we bought a house. Our very first one ever. It was a three-

CRY

bedroom blonde brick detached house in an outer Canberra suburb, Spence. Shelby had one room, Mike and I the master, and the third he used as his 'Study' (Where he turned the built-in-robe into a bank of computer hard drives, I should have guessed what he did that for!) Naturally, there was excitement with owning our own home. Mike built a pergola out in the back garden, and we painted the hallway end entrance a lovely shade of pale blue, all things you just can't do in a rented property. We paid $190,000 for it, taking out a 95% mortgage. With the six grand I had saved, we were, once the Legal fees etc had been added, still five grand short. Step up Shelby, who still had most of her moped accident compensation in the Bank. I made sure I paid her every cent back over the next year, but without her, we couldn't have bought that house without her help.

After a year living in that first house, Shelby and I had bought a horse each, and had them on a large block of land about half an hour away. Going to see them, grooming them, and sometimes, Shelby riding hers, every day or every second day, became too much travelling. Then, one Saturday, in the Classifieds section of The Canberra Times, was an advert for a 43 acre block of land for $73,000. Mike and I travelled to Murrumbateman, about an hour outside of Canberra, to have a look. Situated at the top of a mountain road, with a good portion of the road been un-made, and full of pot holes, we stood at the gate and marveled at the peace and quiet of it all, The Block itself was mountainous and rocky, and full of eucalypt trees, but there wasn't another person to be seen, and the peace and quiet was phenomenal. There as a good-sized dam filled with water and the electricity had been put on up to the gate. All we had to do was to pay to have another electricity pole brought up to the house site, which we did. There was a building site cut out, ready for a house to be built on. I fell in love with it, Mike, going along for the ride, as per usual, not adding anything. We bought the land, using the equity in our house, then put the house on the market. It sold on the first weekend for $200,000, an $80,000 profit in twelve months. While we waited for Settlement, we bought Home Building magazines, and came across a really lovely Kit Home. It was, we found out, to cost us around $60,000 to have it erected. A friend of mine told me that we would be better off taking the picture of the Kit Home to an Architect and get him to design one similar for us. That way we could 'tweak' bits and pieces as needed. So that's what we did. When we had to move out of Spence when it had Settled, and the new owners wanted to move in, we had found a builder, as we now had Plans, and had done the compulsory Planning Application to the local Yass Council for Planning Permission. But where to live while the house was being built? I came up with an idea. Why not hire a caravan and a port-a-loo and actually live on the land itself? I couldn't wait to get there, and even though we would have a daily commute back to Canberra for work, it didn't faze me. We soon found a small caravan for a cheap rent, and

CRY

a company who provided us with a rented port-a-loo. We were to spend the next nine months living there like that. I can remember the excitement every evening coming home from work to see what had been done on the build that day. I had to choose tiles, Colourbond colors, bath, showers, toilets, I had the builder widen the windows and doors, so that almost the entire frontage of our new house would be glass, I chose Oak doors and window frames, pine flooring, I had curtains made, solid brass door handles, ultra-modern taps, even the kitchen sink. Everything. And it was one of the happiest times of my life. Mike and I, now with a common purpose, got on a lot better, although still not intimately or emotionally (he was incapable of either) but we really did enjoy building that house together. Come the day, nine months later, when the Builder was supposed to sign off on the job, and hand us the keys, we were really excited. But before he would give us the them, he demanded another $25,000. What on earth for? I asked him. Apparently, every time I had asked him to make a change to the door and window widths (so we could have more glass), there was a charge. The same with changing the door and window frames from steel or aluminum to wood. Now, at no time during the entire build, did he even mention that there would be an extra charge to do this or that. I did tell him that but he wasn't interested. So, the following day, we had to go back to the Bank and ask for the extra money. Luckily, we got it and then the keys. All in all, we had a stunning mountain top house, with a gorgeous glass frontage and one of the biggest living areas I had ever seen. It really was gorgeous, but somehow, I didn't think I deserved it.

During the latter half of the build, Mike and our sons Stuart and Leo, had all helped to build a double garage. Mike had put in a separating wall and we moved out of the caravan into the far side of the garage, which was insulated and contained our bed, two short bookcases, back to back, our TV on one side and all of the kitchen things on the other. On the other side of the partition we kept some belongings. We were later to buy new furniture when the house was finished. We had no water, electricity, or proper toilet (Sound familiar? Herne Bay in Kent?) We would fill up two large plastic containers every day with water from our son's house after we'd finished work, bought a generator, until we could get the electricity brought up to the house site and switched on. (The day that happened was like winning the lottery). However, there was, I found out, a down-side to living in the bush. Mice were to plague our time living in the garage. I can't bear the rodents and I was petrified of them. We even had a bloody big rat on the ceiling (yes!) one day. I am beyond terrified of these creatures (it's the tails that get me the most!) so we put traps and baits down, but still they kept appearing. When the house was finally built, and we moved the bed etc. out of the garage, we found half a dozen of the creatures, dead, two under our bed. The thought that I had been sleeping on top of them, upset me greatly, and worried me for weeks. (Silly, I know!) We had a sign made up

CRY

for the gate (where the damn was set next to it) for the name of the property 'LITTLE MOUNTAIN'. It seemed fitting. Had we finally found our forever home at last?

TRUE LOVE

Of course we hadn't. You should know me by now, however, you can be still be proud of me! We stayed there for five years from 2002 to 2007, the longest we had ever stayed anywhere. In August of 2002, Shelby became a single mother. She had only known the baby's father for a few months, and had split up with him, before finding herself pregnant a short while later. From the very beginning, in the womb, Julia was to be my baby. When we thought that Shelby had miscarried the baby at twenty weeks, I was completely distraught,

I could barely get out of bed. But, no, all turned out well, and after a difficult pregnancy, on 15th August 2002, my precious girl, Julia, was born by C-Section, weighing in at a hefty 9lb7oz. No wonder the pregnancy was so difficult. As Shelby had all but passed out after the delivery, Julia was put into my waiting arms, and instantly became the only person, other than my grandma, that I had every really felt love for, in a physical way, (Naturally I have loved my own children, but Julia filled my empty heart with something resembling true love) The first few days after her birth, I would walk her all around the hospital in their really old brown pram, taking in the admiring glances, as proud as it is possible to be. For some reason, Shelby wasn't that interested in Julia, and to all intents and purposes, she was my baby. I worshipped her. Adored her like no other, and spoilt her rotten. She stayed with Mike and I up at Little Mountain for most of the time, while Shelby continued with her life of going out to Karaoke and talking on Messenger on her phone to far-away 'friends'. After a short while, I decided to go back to work, part-time (I'd quit my last job just before Julia was born), and Shelby had to look after her during the days when I worked. But somehow, Shelby just wasn't cut out to be a Mum. I'm sure she tried, but just couldn't get it right. One day, when Julia was about 6-8 weeks old, Shelby rang me and, crying, told me she was pregnant again. The father was the same man who had fathered Julia, a waste of space, who thought of nothing but his own needs, his pot smoking and his Pub social life. To this day, we call him 'The

CRY

Sperm Donor, as he has only ever seen both children about three time in their lives, and not for many years now, and had never wanted anything to do with either Shelby or his two children. Having got a dose of the 'baby blues', Shelby had contacted him, told him of their new daughter, and he had gone to her house to see Julia for himself. He was to stay just four days, but it only takes a few minutes to make a baby, and that's what had happened. Shelby was to become a single mum for the second time in eleven months. Cue the 'sperm doner' to disappear as fast as he could! I have to admit, I mostly ignored that second pregnancy, and with a deep feeling of dread. Shelby couldn't look after one child let alone two. So I buried my head in the sand, until come the day James' birth was to be induced, as Mike, Julia and I drove on the approach road to the hospital, I was almost sick as it struck me what was about to happen. James was born at the same hospital as Julia, again by C-Section, but this time, Shelby seemed to be more interested in him. He was a sickly baby, always with a bad chest, and Shelby would never let me bring him to Little Mountain, as she said the dirt road was not good for his chest. Instead she put him, and then Julia, into day care. From early in the morning until last thing in the evening, those two children, when not with Mike and I, were always in daycare. What did Shelby do with herself all day? Who knows. Every time she went into a Psychiatric Hospital, which was often, Mike and I would have to have both James and Julia, as well as holding down full-time jobs (Yes, I'd started at yet another Real Estate Agency full time!), picking the children up from Daycare at 6pm, driving the hour back to Little Mountain, feed them, bath them, I'd tell them a story, then bed, only to have to get up again at six the next day and do it all over again. Weekends were easier, of course, and we would take them both to a large play center in Canberra, and on other little outings. I taught Julia to read at 10 months, and both she and James, when Shelby eventually allowed him to come to Little Mountain a year later, seemed very settled with us.

One feature of Mike's and my life together, and one of the only ways when we were, in a way, reasonably happy, was when we went on holidays. I must admit that planning and booking our trips away were better than the actual holiday for me. For instance, going to Egypt on our 25th Anniversary was somewhere I'm so glad I visited, but wouldn't want to go again (even if it were possible in 2020 with the Pandemic!) We arrived at Cairo airport almost at midnight. The airport itself surprised me. It was a small rectangular building with, I think, just one Departure Lounge and very little in the of refreshments, so unlike other airports around the world. Being on an escorted Tour, there was a coach waiting outside for our group and we made our way to Giza, where not only our Hotel was located, but also the famous Sphinx and the Pyramids. I noticed that there were a lot of people out in the street, men, women, children and dogs. They sat everywhere: in the median strip, on the banks at the side of the main

CRY

roads, everywhere. The reason for this, our Tour Guide told us, was that at this time of night, it was cool enough for people to go out and socialize, the daytime being too hot. That didn't bode well for me as I hate the heat. We arrived at the Hotel (the pool was green!) and before being shown to our rooms, we were warned about the taxi drivers. There would be dozens of them, outside the Hotel, in the morning, we were told, and all would fight for our business. The Guide told us to pick just ONE Taxi Driver, and stay with him for the whole week. Our room was awful and the air conditioning didn't work. After much protest, we were moved to another room with working (although decrepit) air conditioning. The following morning, after virtually no sleep as it was too hot, even with the air on, and the traffic noise outside, which persisted right throughout the night, we made our way out of the Hotel. Greeting us must have been at least two dozen taxis and their drivers, all shouting at us to get out attention. One, more forceful than the others told us to come around the corner to his taxi. Remembering the words of our Tour Guide to stick to just the one driver, we went with him. He continued shooing all of the other drivers away, and told us his name was Sabbah. Once we arrived at his taxi, a run-down old green monstrosity, he pulled from the front passenger seat an old photo album, which he insisted we look at. It was full, page after page, of scraps and sheets of paper and thin cardboard. All had glowing references hand written on them; Sabbah is the best driver in Egypt." "Sabbah is a very careful driver, he's great."

etc. There were dozens of them, all in the same vein. We got in the taxi and asked to go to the Mena Hotel, where we were going to spend the day (It was, at the time, the best Hotel in Giza, overlooking the Pyramids. "I will just take you to my cousin's first. He makes lovely perfume." No thank you, Sabbah. "Oh, it's Ok. It's on our way there. It won't take long." The cousin's perfume 'shop' was a sight to behold. It was a massive room fitted with luxurious red carpet and long, flowing silk drapes at the windows, and beautifully upholstered chairs, which we were invited to sit on. A young man, in Egyptian dress asked us "Tea? Coffee? Coca Cola?" After the cokes were brought to us, on a silver platter mind, then came the real business of the day. A tall, well-built man, in an exotic and extremely colorful costume, complete with an 'over-the-top' silk turban, arrived. With some difficulty, he actually knelt before Mike and I. He held a wooden box, beautifully engraved and opened it with a flourish. Inside was dozens of small bottles of perfume, which Turban Man started to take out, and smear a little onto my arm. After about the third one, they all started to smell the same. Wanting to get out and get to the Mena Hotel, I chose the next one he showed me. Right. We can go now. But no. "Look over there", he pointed. "Choose which bottle you like best and we will fill it with this exotic perfume for you". Unbelievably, and somewhat ironically, Turban Man nudged Mike in the ribs and said in his sexiest voice, "Who know, you might get bit of action tonight hey! Ha Ha". I think this may have been lost on Mike though! Yeah? When I looked, I

CRY

hadn't noticed the wall with Ceiling to floor glass cabinets mounted on it. There were literally hundreds of the most exquisite perfume bottles, pinks, purples, pale blues and greens, absolutely stunning, like fine cut crystal. I chose a beautiful pink one and just before Turban Man sent it to be filled, I thought I'd better ask the price, because up until now, no prices had been mentioned. After consulting his book, Turban Man informed me that it would 'only' be the equivalent of around a thousand pounds! Oh, my heavens, said I. I can't afford that. "What can you afford?" says Turban Man. About a hundred Egyptian pounds says I, the equivalent of about a pound. He tried. I'll give him that. He tried and tried, but, as they say, 'you can't sell to a salesman' and we left the shop with me carrying a tiny vial of the perfume that would send Mike wild in the bedroom that night! Ha! Sorry, I can't stop laughing at the thought of a 'WILD' Mike in the bedroom! Me, smothered in the perfume (the amount in the tiny vial would have just covered my little finger. Maybe Mike might have a finger fetish? I maybe should have asked him that back in 1967 yes? Sorry!

The rest of our Egypt trip was a real eye opener. The Pyramids and the Sphinx, well, you won't see anything like them in the world. And when we went down the River Nile, we saw children playing and mothers washing clothes all in the same water as giant buffalo, it was mind boggling. There are no words to describe the difference in cultures with other parts of the world. For instance, did you know that in Egypt, many buildings don't have rooves. That is because if you put a roof on a house, you have to pay taxes. The majority of the people there would also sleep on the top of these roofless buildings to try and stay cool Unfortunately though, when we went in '93, the country was extremely poor, and the only thing the Egyptians were interested in was getting whatever money that could off you.so we bought a lot of 'tatt' back home with us. Sabbah, our Taxi Driver, did stay with us for our whole week in Giza. When it came to our final day there, I asked him how much we owned him. (He hadn't yet charged us during the week we'd been with him) He just said "Whatever you like", which was pretty hard, as we didn't have a clue. As we'd had him every day, all week, I think we gave him twenty pounds. But on our back to our Hotel with him, he had one last ace up his sleeve. "I must finally take you to my brother who grows Mangoes". No, no, thank you Sabbah. We fly to Luxor tomorrow. We don't need Mangoes. "No, no, it's on our way". We pulled up to a treed Mango Grove where, inside, sat a family on the dirt floor. The only other things there were a small wooden table and a set of weighing scales. Sabbah called his brother (who knows if he was or not?) over and in their own language said something I didn't understand. The brother then started to pile in about a dozen ripe Mangoes into a plastic bag, but not before weighing them. Sabbah put out his hand and asked for money (I can't remember how much, but it wasn't a lot). Even though we were flying out to Luxor to start our Nile Cruise the next morning, I just didn't have the

CRY

heart not to pay for the Mangoes. This poor family would be relying on tourists like us to probably stay alive, so I handed over my Egyptian pounds willingly. Back at the Hotel, I think we ate one each, then threw the rest in the bin. At the end of that final taxi ride, I had asked Sabbah how much we owed him (don't forget we'd had him all week) and he just said 'Whatever you think!" That was really hard as we had no idea how much to give him. Eventually I gave him sixty Egyptian pounds and he thanked us. I will never know if I gave him enough or too much. One final tit bit to end this story was that on the last day with him, Sabbah had said to me "You have sister?" I told him I had two. "They marry?" I told him one was, the other not. He asked me if he could travel over to meet her, and if he thought she looked like me (??) then he would arrange with the Egyptian Embassy for her to come over and be his third wife, as he was looking for one. My sister, and I, when we returned to the UK, had weeks of hilarity over this! While we were still on the Nile Cruise, a few days before it ended, I became sick. I itched from head to toe and felt rally ill, so I had to miss some of the daily excursions and spent the majority of the time in my cabin, standing under a cool shower (to stop the itching and burning skin. On the day when we were due to leave, Mike and I were all packed and standing with our cases by the Exit on the boat. We had been the usual Tourists and had bought lots of cheap 'tat' from the Egyptians, mostly children, but some men and women (when I went to the public toilet at Luxor, I had to pay two Egyptian pounds just to enter. The native woman inside then 'sold' me ONE square of toilet paper and I had to pay her for some more. (Expensive business, doing a pee in Luxor!) When we were back home in England, I immediately visited my Doctor, who said I'd had Liver Failure. I asked how I could have got this, but he didn't know. Anyway, as I said, I'm glad I went, as it is just so removed from the Western World, but never again.

THE TRAVEL BUG STRIKES AGAIN

With my own four children now all grown up, and two good incomes coming in from our jobs, I decided that Mike and I would go on a Tour of Italy. We'd previously been to Paris a few times while we'd lived in England,

CRY

but, having done a Bachelor of Arts in the 80s, studying Art History, amongst other things, I thought how nice it would be to see the paintings, the Vatican and Lake Como. So we flew to London two weeks before the Tour was due to start, and visited relatives, and played the part of 'Sightseer'. We then flew to Milan, where we were supposed to be greeted by a Guide, who would take us in to Baveno, our first stop. But there was nobody there to meet us, so after waiting for two hours, I found an Information Desk and in the best way I could, as I can't speak a word of Italian, asked how to get to Baveno. The man behind the counter pointed outside where a line of buses sat, and said "Number 5". We got on the Number 5, which, we found out, took us to the center of Milan, and the main Railway Station. We got off the bus and walked over to a line of waiting taxis. I showed the driver a piece of paper with the address of where we needed to go, to meet up with the rest of the Tour and its Director, and he said something in Italian that we didn't understand. We drove around for about fifteen minutes, me marveling at the City itself, although not too different from the many other Cities around the world I had already seen (Paris, Bath, Bruges, York, New York, LA.) I thought it beautiful. Suddenly the taxi driver pulled over and told us in broken English, that we should get out and walk down a side street, as he thought that was where we needed to go. The side street he sent us down was indeed the name of the street our Hotel was on, but there was no Hotel. We emerged onto a main street and I attempted, without success, to find someone who spoke English. Stranded in the middle of a strange City, unable to speak a word of the language, and lost. Great. I asked Mike what we should do. He just shrugged his shoulders and said "I don't know". A youngish man was approaching, dressed in an immaculate business suit and carrying a briefcase. Decided to have one last go and amazingly, his English was almost perfect. When I showed him the piece of paper with the address in Baveno on it. Imagine our anger when, he told us the Baveno we wanted was over two hours away. He pointed the Railway Station out and told us to go there and get a train. We had been walking the street in Milan for almost two hours, pulling our suitcases over cobbled streets, (the wheels had broken on my case). I was angry with both the man at the Reception Desk at the Airport, and with the bus driver, both who had given us absolutely the wrong directions. After navigating the Arrivals and Departure Boards at the Station, all in Italian, of course, I managed to buy two tickets and asked which platform. Unfortunately, I didn't understand a word the ticket seller said so we walked up and down the dozen or so platforms trying to find the word 'Baveno', At last, an elderly woman understood me when I asked her, and soon we were on the (hopefully – I was sick with nerves in case it wasn't the right train!) right train. But, I remembered, we were two hours away. How would we tell when it was out stop coming up? So I walked up and down the carriage, (which mostly held schoolboys for some reason), but none spoke any

CRY

English. Then finally, in the next carriage, a lady told me in broken English the name of the Station BEFORE Baveno. All I need to do was keep my eyes open for that one. She also told me it was 'a long way away'. Suddenly, I was furious with our Travel Agent back in Canberra. She had told us there would be someone at Milan Airport, but nobody had shown up in the two hours we'd waited. I decided to phone her later when we were at the Hotel, that evening. Eventually, the train pulled into Baveno. Mike and I had already got up and stood by the door with our heavy cases. But the door didn't open. Panic. The train had stopped completely. But no door opened. Mike manually, and with some force, pulled the doors open a fraction, and I threw out the suitcases and squeezed through the narrow opening, followed by Mike. To top the day off, we made our way over the bridge to the other side of the Station, where there was a waiting Taxi. We gladly climbed in, "Hotel Dino, please". Certainly. The driver turned the car around, and drove over the road. In front of us as the Hotel Dino, He had the cheek to charge us twenty Euros.

After a wonderful trip around Italy, (if you haven't been and get the chance, do go. Naturally there are the bad parts, but the history, and particularly Venice and the Vatican really were worth the trip) Even after such a bad start, we enjoyed Italy (well I know I did) a lot and I vowed to take Julia there with me one day. However, it was now back to business as usual at home. With having to care for Shelby's two babies, who were just eleven months apart, Mike and I had no time for thoughts of ourselves, (although he says he never thought about our life together. He just 'did' it!) By now I was fifty and I had long held plans to have left Mike by this stage in my life, and to start afresh. I was still very overweight and disliked myself intensely, and had become so used to the lack of attention, love and affection, that I just 'lived', doing what I had to with the children. Luckily, my boys had all flown the nest and had settled down, Stuart in a good IT job, married with 3 glorious grandchildren, Mark, a photographer and IT specialist, with three children of his own, and Leo, still single, but a bit of a 'ladies' man' who was working on the Open Face Coal mines in Queensland. (Ive told you that he had bought a two-hundred-year old farmhouse in Northern Italy where it is his intention to live 'off the land' when he can). Life, at this stage for both Mike and I, should have become settled, used to each other, and preparing to live out our lives as best we can. Right? Wrong. We moved yet again, (Little Mountain was too far away from our jobs, and with James and Julia as toddlers, life and all the travelling became too draining). So we sold Little Mountain, making a 100% profit on it, and bought a 70's icon of a house in Canberra. It had arches, an original kitchen and bathroom, and best of all, the last owner, who had lived there since it had been built in the 1970s, proudly told me that the brown shag-pile carpet had never had to be cleaned! Ummm. Lovely. But within an hour of Settlement, we'd got the keys off the Solicitor, and I

CRY

had a team of builders (I used those guys all the time at work when I needed any maintenance done on any of the properties I looked after, and so they were doing the work for half what it should have cost), knocking down the arches, making them square and more modern, ripping up the 40-year old 'never cleaned' carpet, then eventually had it transformed into the house of my dreams. In the end, it really was gorgeous. All cream carpets and walls, downlights, and Italian tiles in the kitchen. I was Ok for a while. Mike had been at his Public Service IT job for ten years and I was still doing property management, but still looking after James and Julia moat of the time, as Shelby continued to go in and out of psychiatric hospitals. But you know me! Within a year, Mike and I, along with Shelby, started to talk about coming back to live in England. Shelby wanted to 'make a fresh start', and, ever on the lookout for something to look forward to, I agreed. Mike wouldn't have said no if his life had depended on it. Once we had decided to move back, we arranged for an Auction Company to come in and Auction off everything, we possessed. (It's amazing what people will buy!), apart from what we'd already sent over the week before. Over the years both Mike and I had collected various thing: Prime Minister's Signatures, a Fist Edition of a SIGNED Agatha Christie book, and many more things, all of our furniture, my collection of forty Cabbage Patch dolls, (which I'd bought as an Investment for Julia), Mike's hundreds of pocket-watches that I knew nothing about, and was shocked to see them being brought out for sale on

Auction day (he had kept them well hidden, for some reason. I certainly wouldn't have minded, as I was an avid collector myself!) as well as our car. The Auction itself, having been heavily publicized (Canberra people like a good Auction.) was well attended. After about four hours of the Auction, we all left the house just before the it finished and returned about an hour and a half later. Oh my heavens! I couldn't believe my eyes. The place was stripped bare. Only the carpets remained. We had sent onwards to England a few boxes of possessions, photos, Mike's precious computer and other bits and pieces, but basically, we were now homeless (the house had been sold three weeks before, again at a huge profit due to all the work I'd had done to it) and the new people were moving in the following day. So we said goodbye to my lovely house and went and stayed in a Motel for two nights until our flight to London. We were on the move again. There are two words you can find in the English Dictionary; 'Settle' and 'Down'. I somehow don't think whoever wrote those words was thinking of me at the time!

AIR MILES?

CRY

After a very long flight, (we did stop-over in Dubai for the night but it was too hot, with no air at all, to leave the Hotel) we once again landed at Heathrow. (We could have all been wearing Qantas Uniforms, we were there so often. Mike and I, with Shelby, and her four and five-year old children, James and Julia. We'd pre-booked a people carrier to be picked up at Heathrow airport (which wouldn't start when we arrived there!) and intended to drive back up to York, as Mike had been speaking to a firm that had basically promised to employ him, in Leeds. As we'd lived in York for five years before, we thought it a good idea to go back there, as we knew the area well. But we barely got there. Firstly, Mike had to stop driving at the first motorway services, saying he couldn't keep driving, so I took over, but couldn't keep my eyes open either, so, and goodness knows how she did it, but Shelby took over the driving and somehow got us up to Malton in North Yorkshire, where we had arranged to stay in a farmhouse until we could find more long-term (Me? Long term?) accommodation for both Shelby and the kids and Mike and I. Behind the lovely Farmhouse was a Piggery. James and Julia were there at every opportunity. The pigs themselves were all babies, about six weeks old and the farmer told us that in a few weeks' time they were to be slaughtered for the supermarkets. The kids were mortified. After we had been in the farmhouse for four weeks, we found two properties in the same village. A three-bedroom house, which we had to pay four weeks Bond and THREE months' rent (we had no rental references) on both properties. Shelby and the children had the three-bedroom house, and Mike and I had a, well, don't really know what to call it, but it was a two-story building, tacked onto the end of the Estate Office, it being neither a house or a flat. Being late November and December, it was bitterly cold. We had just come from the middle of the Australian summer, arriving in the middle of the bitterly cold English winter. Never venturing outside very often is quite normal surely? Isn't it?

Mike soon found a job dealing with the computers at a senior school, (the Leeds job had come to nothing!) but I mooched around the house, watching repeats of Coronation Street and listening to the local York Radio. We bought Shelby a car, and Mike and I a Renault people carrier each. A red one for him and a blue one for me (We are both avid Liverpool FC supporters, so I had to drive the blue one with good grace! NOT!) So, with nothing to do all day, and it being too bitterly cold to go out anywhere, I somehow got it into my head that there was something I could enjoy doing. After a bit of research, I decided I would become a Magistrate. In the mid 80s, I had applied to the Australian National University to study Law, but with so many applicants that year, they had had to be really choosy, but had offered me to undertake a Bachelor of Arts instead, which I did, in History and Fine Art, but still the Law appealed to me. It seemed that all I had to do was to have a clean Police Record: tick, and attend three Court Sessions in Scarborough

CRY

Local Court: tick. The next step was that I would sit on the bench with a Senior Magistrate and a Junior one, and learn the ropes. Having always hankered to become a Lawyer, I thought this the ideal thing to do. "Send him Down" was something I longed to say. (No, not really!!). But then one day, Mike and I were watching evening TV, and there was a program on about British people who had emigrated to Australia, came back over to the UK to live, but had regretted doing so, and went back to live in Australia. Something hit a nerve, and I immediately rang Shelby, told her about the program I'd seen on TV, and said
"I want to go back"! Shelby nearly jumped down the 'phone.
"So do I, Mum. I hate it here." Gee, this is getting ridicules, yes? So once again, the following morning, and without even bothering to consult Mike, as he would have just gone along with whatever we did anyway, I booked us all on a Singapore Airlines one-way flight back to Sydney, then on to Canberra. We had been away for exactly three months and two weeks. Bang went my chance of sitting on the Bench. Two weeks later, when the time came for us to leave, we actually had to 'Do a Runner', as both Shelby and Mike and I had two year Leases on our houses. We left on a Saturday morning, a time when we thought nobody would notice the large Removal Van which came to take our ten thousand pounds' worth of expensive furniture (WHY?) and household things to an Auction House to await the next Auction. (They promised to send whatever money our things made

over to our bank.) In what was to be a very annoying situation, it was impossible to sell furniture and other goods, unlike here in Canberra, where you can buy and sell anything. So, after finding out that there was nowhere to sell our almost brand new, expensive household furniture and goods to, we had no option but to put what would be saleable into the next Auction. That Saturday, we'd packed our clothes and personal belongings and waited. Prior to the Van arriving, I heard a commotion outside and went to look out of the window. Typical! There were we, trying to inconspicuously leg it without anyone seeing us, and it just so happened that on that very day a Hunt was taking place. Very soon, dozens of howling and barking hounds were right outside our house where the Removal Van was due to arrive at any minute. Men dressed in their red Hunting outfits, sitting astride beautifully manicured horses, moseyed around. Oh heavens! Please Van, don't arrive yet. It being lunch time, Mike decided to nip into town to get some pasties. Shelby and I stood at the window begging the Hunt to get moving, please, just go! The two children, who were now five and six, stood whining: "When are we going?" The whole thing was fraught with anxiety. However, eventually the Hunt left to catch up with some poor fox, and almost immediately, the Removal Van drew up, it's air brakes hissing. Mike arrived back with a pasty each, but I couldn't eat mine. I told Shelby to get the children into the Hire car (We had sold all three cars back to the Dealer at a 50% loss. We had them three months) and told the removal man to take everything he thought would sell and we would be back later (of course, we wouldn't be) to sort everything else out. I just wanted to get away, terrified that someone from the adjoining Estate Office would come and see the Van outside. However, the Removalist insisted on going around the house and listing all of the things that could be sold at Auction, with me following him impatiently, just wanting to get away. I had never 'done a runner' in my life before and don't recommend it. (Having made the decision to return to Australia so quickly meant that we hadn't had time to try and sell everything privately. So that's how we came to leave behind lots of really expensive bedding, ornaments, pictures, and all the kids toys, all things that weren't sellable, according to the Removal man) In all, looking after not only ourselves, but Shelby and her two children, financially, and including air fares, that three months living back in a freezing England – heating oil cost us two hundred pounds every two weeks, for both ourselves and Shelby and the kids, was to cost Mike and I $100,000, a big part of our Superannuation. Never again. When would I ever learn?

When we had first emigrated to Australia, way back in 1973, all of my five siblings were living in various places in England. David went out to live for many years in Tenerife with his wife and two children, Peter sold his General Store in Redcar, England, and emigrated himself to Australia, and now lives in Queensland. Anne and Linda are still living in

Birkenhead, and the youngest, Diane is also in Queensland, having been brought over in the late seventies by my Mum and her new husband, Don. Now, with Mike, Shelby and her children and I, also back in Australia, we had decided not to return to the grind of life and work in Canberra. We'd been there since 1981 and work for me at least, was becoming too much, especially given our involvement with Shelby's children. By this time, we were both 56 and Shelby and I wanted a change. As usual, Mike had nothing to impart, and just went along, whatever. We decided to take early retirement and go and live on the South Coast, in the little holiday town of Bateman's Bay which sits on a lovely part of the Pacific Ocean. Over the years, with it only being not quite two hours away from Canberra, we had been down there many times. In the summer, it would be packed with tourists and beachgoers, but in winter, it was dead, and certainly no place for two growing children to be brought up. There's only so many times you can say "let's go to the beach" and to be greeted with the response, "do we have to?" There were plenty of beaches, a shopping center, and all the usual Take-A-Way joints, and of course, the beautiful Pacific Ocean. We enrolled the children into school, but James, who had started having really serious behavioral problems the year before, was constantly being sent home, or worse, suspended. Shelby tried to get support from various organizations, but in the end, it was too much for her, a single mother with mental illness, to cope with. In retrospect, although I wouldn't for one second

CRY

not want James and Julia here today, Shelby should never have been a mother. It wasn't her fault, but some women have a maternal instinct. Unfortunately, Shelby wasn't one of those women back in those early days. (She's great now though!) The children fought and fought in her care. I bought them thousands of dollars worth of toys, games, and clothes, but Shelby would throw them out as they 'got under her feet', so I'd go out and buy more, only for it to happen all over again. The lack of attention the kids received while with Shelby caused them to constantly fight with each other, having nothing else to stimulate themselves, It was also around this time that she had some new treatment for her mental health, which eventually would prove to work wonders. However, DOCS (our Social Services) after many Reports from various people and organisations, realized that Shelby was unable to care for her children and put both James and Julia into Mike's and my Care full time. So, at an age when we should have been planning for our future retirement, (and for me to put my grand Plan of leaving ALONE, into action, which I had worked out a year or so earlier, would now have to be again put on hold. I'd always thought that money, or lack of enough of it, was the deciding factor, but I was starting to realize that Mike had some kind of weird hold over me. I can't quite describe it, nor put my finger on it, but something, I don't know what (and it certainly wasn't love or affection) had continually stopped me from leaving him, when I so desperately wanted to over the years. I felt as though I wanted to 'Run for the Hills', something I should have done 45 years ago, but we now had to become parents again to a naughty six-year old boy (naughty doesn't even begin to cover James' behavior) and my seven-year old precious girl, Julia. I did what I could with them, Mike taking on the part of the 'Driver' when we went out, and eventually they stopped their fighting and hitting each other, and started reading and playing games, something which calmed them both down, and they easily settled down with us as we were a very big part of their lives and had been since their birth. But still, at school, as well as at home, James behavior was out of control. DOCS sent us to Sydney to a type of 'parenting' school, so that we could learn how to handle James. I can remember the Report given at the end of our week there, which said "Trish is bonded really well with both children, and is fair and loving. The children love her very much, and we are sure that under her care, James and Julia will thrive". The same could not, however, be said about Mikes Report. It went something like "The children's grandfather does not have much of a connection with either child. He needs to communicate and play with them more, especially James, who desperately needs a strong male role model in his life" Ha! They had to be joking! A 'strong male role model' I might as well have gone and picked up a guy off the street So there you have it. Finally, somebody else had acknowledged everything I'd thought and said for the past 45 years. I was glad that Mike had been finally 'outed', although it gave me no pleasure whatsoever that there was someone else

CRY

who had agreed with me. While we were there, Mike was taught how to safely restrain James when he was having a 'tantrum' (for want of a better word!), and it was a technique he would have to use quite a few times over the next three years. (I might say at this point, the children's 'father' – who we actually call 'The Sperm Doner' had never been interested in being part of his children's life. He paid no Child Support, sent no cards for birthdays or Christmas. Nothing. Shelby, having had her children taken off her, retreated into herself, and for a while she and I, usually so close, didn't really talk. Every weekend, the only thing available to do we could do, once the initial novelty of the beach wore off, and in the winter months especially, was to drive almost an hour each way to the next town, Ulladulla, where there was both an indoor swimming pool, and an Amusement Arcade, with various games and things to do. Boy, did I get tired of doing that journey most weekends for five years.

Batemans Bay is about a two-hour drive, up a very steep mountain, The Clyde, back to Canberra, where my two sons and my other grandchildren lived. We would do this journey about once a month, get everyone together and go to a club and have a meal and catch up. But after five years, it all got too much, and yes, you guessed it, we decided to move back. (You must remember that Mike couldn't have cared less where we lived, so when I say "we' moved, naturally it was either myself, or sometimes with

Shelby, never Mike, who just agreed to everything) Neither of the children were settled in school, especially James who had been sent to another school with a special class for children with any kind of major behavioral problems, (The school was almost an hour away, and at first, he could only go for two hours at a time, so Mike and I would have to sit in a local Café, waiting, as to go home would have meant an immediate turn-around to go back and get him) and amazingly, the previously good Julia also started playing up and was constantly having to be picked up from her school. Instead of living in Canberra, where Mike and I wouldn't have received the Social Services Carers Allowance, which we badly needed to make ends meet, especially with the high rents in the Canberra area, so we had to stay across the Border. We rented a house in Queanbeyan, which is in New South Wales, minutes away from Canberra, and where we would get the Allowance. (Queanbeyan is a large Town on the border with Canberra, and is almost a suburb. I can get into Canberra from where I now live within minutes) However, yet again, at his new school, James was constantly suspended, then expelled. He had a temper like I had never seen before and a tongue as sharp as his fists. We constantly walked on eggshells with him for fear of setting him off, and I had to hide all the knives and scissors in the house, that's how afraid we all were of him. I would hide the new scissors he'd bring home from school one day, only for him to bring another pair home the following day. My own belief is that he had never had a father figure in

CRY

his life. Mike was like a marshmallow, and James could barely get a word out of him. He was a real 'boy', and desperately needed another 'man' to connect with, play footy with, rough and tumble and more importantly, discipline him. Naturally I would chastise him, but I was just 'a woman' and James had no respect for them. But every night, regardless of how he had behaved, when he was in bed, I would 'tickle' his back and tell him how much I loved him. (This closeness would mean that James, even with all he's been through since I put him into Care, still sees or rings me every day. Nobody else, just me, and I love him dearly) By the time he had been in our Care for four years, I decided enough was enough. Mike wasn't getting any younger, or stronger, while James was. Remember those restraining techniques Mike had been taught in Sydney years ago? Well they came into play quite a few times. I had to call the Police on more than one occasion, with poor Julia standing out in the street screaming, while Mike held down a foul-mouthed, kicking and fighting, James. Not only did we have to cope with the violence, but James had a mouth on him that a docker would have been proud of. Soon there was only one thing I could do. I had to put him in Care. He would destroy a room in minutes. I was also always very afraid for Julia, as I sensed a deep hatred and jealousy for her from him. So, I contacted DOCS and went to Court to have him placed in 'The Care of the Minister until he turns 18'. It was a horrible time, as, believe it or not, I really did love him, and I knew that his behavior wasn't his fault.

Along with James, also went his quite substantial fortnightly allowance, so yet again, we had to move, as the rent on our house was now unaffordable. Now, with just Julia and I almost stuck together at the hip, I decided that this would be a good as time as any to finally do what I should have done many years ago, 'The Plan", and that was to leave Mike, who by the way, had, over the many years we'd been married, had changed not one iota from the 16-year old boy I had met in 1967. We hadn't had any sort of sex or intimacy in many, many years, he barely ever spoke, other than about the absolute necessities of life, ("What are we having for tea? Coronation Street's on that USB", you get the picture) and I now knew nothing of any private life he may have had. If he was watching or using pornography, I no longer knew about it. Occasionally, in desperation, I would try and get a cuddle, but if he gave it, I just knew there was love or emotion, no feeling whatsoever, behind it, and he would be like a block of stone, and quickly pull away. So here we are again packing up for the gazillionth time. We packed up, and moved an hour away, to the much cheaper suburb of Yass, about an hour outside of Canberra, and not too far from where we'd built our lovely house 'Little Mountain' My poor darling James? He was shipped off to the South Coast to a Care Home. A few days after the Court Hearing, he rang me. "Nan, did you agree to me not living with you anymore?" There was only one answer I could give him; the truth. "Yes darlin', I did."

CRY

A NEW PROFESSION

The house at Yass was brand new and in a little cul-de-sac of eight other houses, all the same. Being new, it was really modern and, having money left over from mostly our superannuation, we bought a matching set of beautiful cream-colored furniture. We had our dog, a cream poodle named Hamish and I bought another six-week old puppy, Angus, a mixed-breed Cavalier King Charles Spaniel and Maltese. (Somehow, Angus is absolutely NOTHING like either of these breeds and I think the breeder saw us coming.) I had become a member of a Facebook Site, Birkenhead Memories, and for some reason, where others were putting old photos of Birkenhead, and asking questions about Birkenhead events etc. on there, I don't know why I started to put snippets of my early life in Birkenhead, just snippets of my early memories of growing up in Birkenhead, on the Site. Certainly, though, nothing personal. I would write no more than a hundred or so words, but where other Posts were getting ten or twelve 'Comments' and 'Likes' at best, I was getting six or seven HUNDRED Comments and Likes. People were soon clambering for more, and eventually I was told by many to write a book' And that is how my very first book, 'A Girl from Birkenhead' came about. I found out that it is free and easy to Publish on Amazon, and I chose a picture for the Cover (One of only two pictures I have of my childhood. I'm in my white Communion dress) and within two days, it was 'live' and available. I was to be blown away by its success, and this spurred me on to publish a book of letters I had, many years ago, transcribed from the actual letters of Mike's grandfather who had died in WW1, to his wife, Alice. I soon published 'Dear Alice' as a follow up to 'A Girl from Birkenhead' then, full of motivation (remember that typewriter my Dad had given me all those years ago?), I made a start on my first novel, a Sun, Sand & Sex saga, set on a tropical, luxury Island Resort in our wonderful Great Barrier Reef area of Northern Queensland, where Mike and I had once visited (Brampton Island) a few years ago, 'Escape to Paradise Island', Now, ME, writing about sex? Well, I have no idea how I did it, but 89,000 words later, I had another hit on my hands, and the royalties poured in. Within a week of the book being published, I was inundated by readers begging me to write another one, so, as easy as spreading butter, I quickly wrote the sequel 'Return to Paradise Island", again to great acclaim. Readers started asking me to make the books into a Movie and I set about researching what I had to do to make this happen.

CRY

Julia, never settled at school, always seeming to not get on and clash with one child or another. One day, I met her outside the school gates (Mike was continuously locked away in the third bedroom, which he used as a study, doing I don't know what, and, as usual, barely spoke to her.) Outside school, she burst into tears. A boy in her class had hit her and she "wasn't going back'. I decided there and then that I would Home School her. Even though I had only finished school at 15, I had, years ago, done a Bachelor of Arts in History, I was good at English, and I knew I could write, but the only thing I knew I wouldn't be able to help her with was Math's. So I contacted the Education Department, who promised to send me work for her to do, with my help, every two weeks. The idea being that she would do the work, send it back via the post, then her work would be returned to her, marked. Both Julia and I were very excited at this at first. That first week, we went down to the National Gallery, the National Museum and Parliament House in Canberra and I did what I could to give her what information I had on various topics. From birth, Julia and I had instantly bonded, if fact she was like my own child. We were, basically, joined at the hip, and for the first time ever in my life, I knew what love meant. Sure, I loved James, and my other grandchildren, but not in the way I loved Julia. I became quite spiritual, and thought that Julia had been 'sent' to me. Finally, I had that love and need that I had been craving all my life. Our Home Schooling packages arrived every fortnight, and at first, Julia and

I would get them finished and sent back. But over the course of the year, Home Schooling Julia became untenable. She was now twelve, and would lay in bed until lunchtime, get up, have something to eat, then do half an hour's school work. I became incredibly frustrated and soon, something had to give. So I was amazed when she announced that she'd like to start at the local High School. I now think that the pressure of getting out of bed and actually doing the Home School work was taking its toll on her as much as it was me. So, with new uniform bought (No red and white diamond socks for my girl!) Julia started in Year 7. But it wasn't to be long before, once again, she was having trouble with other girls in her class and wanted to leave. There being no other High School in Yass, well, you know what's coming! We moved back to Queanbeyan and enrolled her into the local High School there. We rented a lovely house and made yet another 'fresh start'. But what of my plans to leave Mike and go it alone with Julia? With everything that had gone on since we'd moved back from Bateman's Bay, the success of my books, Home Schooling Jade, having to give James up into Care, and still try and keep a relationship with my other children and grandchildren, life had just 'taken over', as it always had, and I'd had little, or no, time to think of myself. Sure, I still wanted to leave him, but there was just too much else going on, so I stayed. I know it's a pathetic excuse, but it's true. I had been with him so long now, and was so used to his peculiar ways, his 'different' personality, his lack of communication and any kind of

CRY

emotional attachment to me or anyone else. I remember that years ago, when I had been working, I would throw dinner parties for my workmates and friends. I had amassed an impressive antiques collection of furniture and 'objects d'art' and liked to show it all off, and a dinner party at home with friends or colleagues was the perfect place to do it. We would start around 7pm (my having cooked a three-course meal) and the bon-homie and general conversation around the table would be entertaining. But by around 11pm, just as people were starting to think about leaving, someone in the group would realize that Mike hadn't said a single word all evening, and they would politely say 'And what do you do, Mike?" He would answer just ONE word: "Computers". I would sit there wanting the ground to swallow me up. Say something else, for God's sake, I'd silently plead! But he didn't. He would just sit there with a soft grin on his face. When everyone had left, I would go mad at him. But it was always to no avail. There was one thing I had learnt about Mike over the years, and that was that he really didn't care what people thought about him. He had no emotional feelings whatsoever, and under any circumstances. He was who he was and he was happy with that, something that prevails still to this day.

With Julia now at High School in Queanbeyan, she was yet again bullied. This time by an Indigenous girl who had a large, extended family, who regularly warned Julia that she was going to die, or be 'bashed'. Julia, once again, would come out of school crying, and I got sick of going to see the headmistress, who did nothing. I did what I should have done years ago. I enrolled her into Shelby's old school in Canberra, a Private Catholic School, and it was here that Julia finally settled down. At the time, I had started writing 'The Office Girls', a novel based on my own time as an Office Junior when I was 15, (if you get it, I am 'Hettie' in the book, and everything she does I REALLY did do, something which I am to this day ashamed of and wish I could do something to repair!) and before getting married. However, before I could finish it, my darling Julia and I went away together on a camp for people with Tourette's Syndrome. I know now that the enclosed Camp, which was up on the Central Coast of Australia, was completely safe. But Julia, who had never, ever been out past tea time before, still hadn't come back to our room by midnight. Naturally I couldn't sleep until she had come back, so I rang her. She was with a group of other teenagers hanging out in one of the halls, chatting and generally doing what teenagers do. I demanded (wrongly, I now know) that she get back to the room immediately, which she did, banging around in temper then going to sleep. However, the following morning, when she woke up, boy did she let me have it. Now Julia had never, ever, spoken a cross word to me in her life. She was my darling, the person I loved most in the world. Remember when I said I hadn't cried for twenty years since my Dad had died, well, Julia's tirade at me caused the dam to burst, all the many years-worth of pent-up emotions, and I was to cry for the next five

CRY

months. I was diagnosed with PTSD and spent 2 weeks in a Private Hospital (where all was going well until I fell over the bedding and broke many bones! But that's another story). Back home, something in Julia had changed. She started to spend every single free moment she had (she was 14 by now) with a boy who was almost 21, and her whole attitude changed. She became a typical, hormonal teenager. Not used to being shouted at, which she did at every opportunity, and worst still, with some sort of perverse pleasure, the usually quiet and unemotional Mike, started to take her side. Soon, life became one long shouting match, this time not just with Mike, but also with Julia. Very quickly, I decided that now was the time to get out. If I no longer had Julia, why stay? My decision was made. I didn't need courage anymore. I was going to go it alone. There would be no turning back this time. My mind was moat definitely made up.

TRISH OLLMAN

ALONE AGAIN, NATURALLY!

Without too much thought of where I'd go or what I'd do, the night before I left, I got a suitcase out of the garage and placed it outside my bedroom door, mainly so that Mike and Julia would see that I was going. Before I go on, I have to say that for at least a year or so, Mike had been a frequent visitor to Julia's bedroom, waiting on her hand and foot. When questioned, he'd say he had been taking her a drink in, or a meal. I was giving her $50 a week pocket money for a few years, and I had recently been trying to get her to do just ONE chore to make her earn that money. With everything I asked her to do, Mike would do it first, and before she had a chance to do it. (not that she probably would have done it anyway. She had taken to spending almost all of her spare time lying in bed, and was, and always had been, spoilt. Both Mike and I were to held responsible for that, each in our

CRY

own different way. She was a typical teenager, and had become extremely lazy, and Mike had a year or so earlier, started waiting on her hand and foot, which did nothing to help her start to gain some independence of her own. Therefore, it was only natural that I became the 'Big Bad Wolf' in trying to get her to do just one chore for her pocket money each week, and she soon became, for the first time in her life, affiliated with the push-over, Mike, and aggressive with me, the one person who had, and still did, loved her more than life itself. When I had placed my leaving suitcase outside my bedroom door, neither one of them had even commented on it. Spurred on by anger, adrenalin and who knows what else, the following morning, when Mike was driving Julia to school (no, she couldn't get the bus like everyone else, 'Saint' Mike, had to drive her the 40 minutes there and back!) I packed what clothes and toiletries I could fit into the suitcase and walked out, leaving my keys on the hall table. At last, I'd done what I had wanted to do so many times, and for so many years. At the time, we had two cars, a rather nice BMW, bought with the royalties from the sales of my Books, and a cheap, small Mercedes. I also had some money in the bank account, to which I'd added Mike as a signatory years ago. (Our Joint Account had virtually nothing in it) My first stop was our Council's Housing office, where, on the dot of nine, I walked in, basically saying "here I am, what have you got for me?". "That's not the way it's done" I was told, and was given the phone numbers of a Women's Refuge and a Centre that helped Homeless Women.

Now, I had enough money to go and rent somewhere privately, but for reasons I don't understand, I didn't. The Woman's Refuge, when I rang them, told me they were full, but took my name and mobile number. The Homeless Centre were much better. They arranged for me to rent a cabin in a Tourist Park, then sent me to apply for Community Housing. After explaining my life, and Mike, to the lovely ladies there, I was told that I had suffered for fifty years from 'Emotional Abuse, which, they said, was on a par with Physical Abuse. I was sent to the local Police Station, who also agreed about the abuse, to get a Police Event Number, which would make it easier for me to get Community Housing. Even though I had money (not a great deal, but enough) in the bank, I was in receipt of a Disability Pension because of having Tourette's Syndrome, so was entitled to apply for Community Housing. The afternoon I left home, I felt lost, alone. This was the first time in my entire life that I had lived alone (although maybe not if you think about it! Emotionally and mentally 'alone' is just as bad!) That afternoon, I was having coffee with Shelby, who had started to be a great support to me a while back, when Julia (who, remember, is Shelby's daughter) rang her. "Is Nan with you?" "Yes". 'Ask her why she's taken our BMW". That was the final straw, and I now knew exactly where Julia's loyalties lay: I, who had given her absolutely everything she could have ever wanted: every sport, possessions, toys, 5 Dance classes a week and all the associated costumes, Horse Riding and Camps, soccer, football, gymnastics, karate, BMX Riding,

CRY

Swimming Coaching at the Australian Institute of Sport, everything, as well as Cruises, Overseas Holidays, but most of all, every single bit of myself. She was the only person on the planet to have ME, my heart. Or to stay with Mike, who throughout her life had barely spoken to her, let alone loved and cared for her, played with her, read to her, helped her through her emotional teenage hormonal years. Had he ever done any of those things with her? Of course not! Now at 16, with him waiting on her hand and foot, allowing her to stay in bed, do no chores and do whatever she wanted, it was an easy choice for her to make. She stayed with him, and I have never felt betrayal so badly.

After I'd left, Mike didn't even contact me to see where I was, or if I was ever coming back. As usual, it was just silence. After my visit to Queanbeyan Housing, I went straight to the bank and took Mike's name off the account so he couldn't touch the money, the majority of which had come from my Book Royalties, I figured that I had left him with some very expensive furniture, all of our household belongings, as well as the Mercedes car, my darling Julia, and Hamish and Angus, our two dogs, as well as the complete detritus of my life, so I was keeping the BMW and the money. I then went into the Support Centre that Housing had told me about. The lady there was wonderful, and for the next fortnight, she daily arranged a cabin in a local Caravan Park for me. It was all paid for but was a bit surreal being on my own after being married for fifty years. Then, out of the blue, my daughter, Shelby, told me to go around to her place as she had a surprise for me. She had cleared her spare bedroom out (no mean feat!) and bought me a double bed, a chest of drawers with a TV on top. I was to move in with her until I was given a Community Housing property. My boys, and other grandchildren all acted as though nothing had happened, and not one of them, other than Shelby, offered any help, support, or rang me to see if I was Ok and if I needed anything. Why? No idea. It's just the way it was. Even though I got on well with them, they both had busy lives and just let me get on with mine. I assume they all preferred to hide their heads in the sand and pretend it hadn't happened. I lived with Shelby, quite comfortably, as she and I got on, and still do, like a house on fire. One day, about four weeks later, I got a phone call from the Community Housing Association, telling me they had a two-bedroom Unit for me. They gave me the address and I went around to see it from the outside. It was up a flight of stairs, but that didn't worry me. When I arrived there, the cleaners were just arriving, as the previous tenant, not a very nice man by all accounts, had just been evicted. I must admit, my heart did sink a little. The previous tenant, (it had taken the Association three years to get him out!) had left the Unit in a really bad way. He'd had two male cats and the carpets throughout were soaked in cat pee, peculiar black marks littered ever wall, and to call it a dump was a fitting description. Still, once the cleaners had finished, I signed the lease and was given the keys, just glad to have a place of my own. I

CRY

was still staying With Shelby, so we took a few days to try and clean the walls, the kitchen and bathroom, better than what the cleaners had done, I bought some, what I thought was matching, white paint, and painted over the hundreds of black marks on every wall. I had been buying odds and ends, and some basic furniture over the weeks since I'd left home and storing it in, of all places, Mike's garage. He even painted some shelves and my bed for me! Very odd, don't you think? With the Unit as it was, I asked for new carpet, which had been soaked in cat pee, and a re-paint, but my request was refused. I moved my things in, but the smell from the carpets was awful. I decided to go my GP and ask him for a letter to give to the Housing Association, saying that the smell was affecting my health (which it was! It was driving me batty!) I used Gumption on the walls, a type of cleaning paste, popular here in Australia, along with the paint. But once it had dried, if you look closely enough, you can see that the white/cream paint is actually not quite the same color, but luckily, you can't notice it unless I point it out to you. And so, began my new life in my new home. Over the months, I did get it looking lovely. Not getting anywhere with the Housing Association with having the pee soaked carpet replaced, I decided to go straight to the top. The owners of my Unit Complex Building, a massive Global Conglomerate, who owned hundreds of properties around the world, and throughout Australia, had their Head Office in Sydney, so one day, a few weeks after moving in, I rang them and asked to speak to the

Housing Manager. He was a lovely young guy, very sympathetic, then disbelieving and shocked that the people who his company were paying to manage their properties were not looking after their tenants. Two days later, a carpet company was measuring my Unit up for new carpet, and a further three days later, it was being laid. I had to go out when they were lifting the old carpet up, the smell, and the bright yellow soaked underlay from the cat pee, was just too bad. But when I got home, and my new carpet was laid, I was content as I was ever to be.

During the year after I left Mike, (it was 2019) I applied for, and got, a Divorce. Even though I still didn't have a sexual bone in my body, or any kind or emotional or physical feelings, I joined an on-line Dating Site. Over the course of the year, I spoke to many, many men who had approached me, (I had taken ten years off my age!) some of them for weeks. Gradually over time, I learnt to trust some of them and during a conversation, would explain why I could never commit to a relationship, as I was basically non-sexual. Sure, maybe if they could wait and be patient with me, there was a chance of intimacy, but I could never promise. Every single time, I would never hear from them again, apart from one guy who said, 'Oh, that's a shame. I wanted to show you my ten-inch thick Dick!" So, with my moods becoming more erratic due to the constant rejection from these men, who, it now seems, really only wanted me for one thing. I started to feel sad almost every single day. I was incredibly sad

CRY

for people who had died, pop stars who were no longer with us, and mostly, sad for my own life and the unhappiness that I had endured from both my parents and from Mike. And mostly, for the wasted life, all fifty years of it, with my failed and unhappy marriage. In other words, I was slowly sinking into a deep depression. During this time, James, having now lived in Care since he was nine, started to become violent, and, after four warnings by a Magistrate, ended up in a Juvenile Detention Center near Sydney. I drove up to visit him every month and it was pretty obvious that there was still a lot of love between us.

Mike and I had been married fifty years. Fifty mostly unhappy years I might add. I've already spoken of his lack of speech, communication, companionship, never giving a shit, or even asking, how I was feeling, even when I was diagnosed with PTSD (Is it any wonder??) some years ago! He wouldn't give any emotional or psychological or intimate support. Sure, after fifty years, you certainly don't expect to have the same level of love and 'feelings' from your spouse that you did when you first got together, but remember, I'd had zilch from the very beginning, so you'd think I would be used to it. But you never get use to neglect. Everyone needs someone, someone more than your children, someone who can give you the love and intimacy that we all need. It's not as if I'm 'High Maintenance", I'm not, but any normal woman expects, at the very least, some form of loving and emotional connection, even if it wanes over the years. But for me, no. I got virtually nothing. My children got virtually nothing, and my grandchildren, well, you get the picture. Now this is the bit I don't understand. After I left Mike and Julia (the love of my life) and found myself a lovely new apartment, furnished it, bought lots of gorgeous little nick knacks, and organized my life into that of a separated woman, I had joined the two Online Dating Sites and was soon talking to quite a few guys, either online, or, once we'd been talking for a week or so, sometimes by phone. I got the idea into my had to find a new man who could give me all the things that Mike hadn't. I had four dates with what appeared to be really nice men, all professionals, all quite good looking and well dressed (I'm fussy!) Initially, I got on famously with all four of them, and I thought, finally, I might have found someone (that's how desperate I was!) but after a few hours where we discovered that we both liked the same things, music, books, films, I felt comfortable enough with them to talk about the fact that sex was "way down the list" for me. Big mistake. Of course, I realize now, that any normal 50ish year old male is going to want sex. (Did you know that a man is at his sexual peak between forty and sixty?) But did I want it?? Not a chance. And under no circumstances. So that would be the last I'd hear from them. I would soldier on, trying to make a connection with yet another man. Same thing happened, again and again, knowing every time, that whatever happened, there was no way I was going to be able to become intimate, however much I liked that man. Certainly, not at first, anyway, maybe never, I just

CRY

didn't know. Maybe, if I'd have found the right man, patient and understanding, just maybe, in time, I could have become intimate, but my past experiences with sex had been highly unsatisfactory and it had been many years since my last experience. Now, during this time, and this is the bit I don't understand, as the year progressed, I became extremely morose, and then depressed. Anybody who had died (especially my grandparents, relatives, and even pop stars) would make me cry. Then the crying turned to sobbing, and then to almost screaming, all over the course of the first six months of this year. I could feel a deep hurt and an ache inside my belly, and living seemed futile. Last year, after leaving Mike, I had been excited to be free of him and looking forward to finding a new relationship, but knowing that would never happen due to my dislike of intimacy made me much, much worse and really sad and resigned to being on my own for the rest of my life. After, by chance, seeing an old black and white clip of them singing, on Shelby's Foxtel (TV) I became obsessed with my teenage Pin-Up Band, The Beach Boys, and started to watch old footage of them, some in black and white, until I knew everything there was to know about them. I became unable to go a day without watching their videos, listening to their music, crying or sobbing the whole time. I bought their Autobiographies and Studio Photos, one signed, online and played their music to the exclusion of all else. Finally, I had no option but to visit my GP as I just wanted to die. He prescribed me anti-depressants, but they never helped. Finally, and in despair, I went back to him and he diagnosed me with having Bipolar 2 (Different to regular Bipolar as you don't get the 'Highs' or Manic, only the 'Lows') My low moments, were to get worse, much worse, in the course of the year before they got better. Luckily, I have a wonderful Doctor and he started me on Lithium, which, as I write is working quite well. I still watch The Beach Boys though! But I can watch and listen without crying now.

During the 20 months since I'd left Mike, he never once contacted me. However, when my mood was really, really low, I would make an excuse to see him (Again, WHY?) He would come around and be his usual self, barely talking, and well, just being him. In the first few months I did think that, in order to win me back, he may have tried to change, but no. Not one iota. Did he think that it was HE who was normal, and perhaps I was the one with the problem? Narcissists do think like that, as that is what my Counsellor has said he is. (He's always the one in the right and it's me always in the wrong!) Apart from anything else which he had going on, I'm was now quite sure that Mike, a Narcissist, never taking responsibility for things that happen in life, could also possibly be on the Autistic Spectrum. It would certainly make sense of his personality and his behavior over the years. The symptoms of both Autism and Narcissism, well, they fitted Mike to a tee. Did he think "Why should I change?" I have no idea. Even though I tried to ask him, he wasn't able to give me an answer. At my

CRY

lowest moments, I would contact Mike and we would meet up, (He ALWAYS acted as though nothing had happened, that I hadn't left him) probably every two weeks or so. I'd 'put up with him' for a few days, then be disappointed that he wasn't acting any differently with me, and he'd leave me alone. Naturally, a leopard doesn't change its spots, I told myself, but I thought, at the time, that my leaving, might have caused him to have a re-think about how he had treated me for the past fifty years. But no, I would see him for a few days, then, annoyed with him and his non-behavior, I would send him dreadful texts, letting out all of my pent-up feelings. But no matter how bad my texts were, another week or so later, we would go through it all again. He seemed not to care, and eventually, he made me feel as though it was me who was in the wrong. Our Divorce, after 52 years together, came through in April 2019. Can you be happy and unbelievably sad at the same time?

**AND IN THE END, THE LOVE YOU SAVE IS EQUAL TO THE LOVE YOU GAVE.
The Beatles.**

So, you now know the 'real' truth behind 'A Girl from Birkenhead'. We both, you and I, must ask ourselves, what exactly was it that I had been searching for all my life? Love, affection, care, acceptance, or just safety? All of the above, I think, but mostly, safe in the knowledge that I was loved and cared for, that I was not alone. Ever since I had got married at 16, I have lived in 39 houses and had 29 jobs. These are certainly not the average numbers for any normal person to experience in a lifetime. I only ever found enjoyment, excitement or acceptance with every change of house or job that I had. It was always me, never Mike, who instigated the moves. He was happy to be tied to my shoelaces and do whatever it was I had decided that we do. Over the last ten years of my marriage, I found that I made myself happy by planning and anticipating holidays. As Mike and I, and sometimes our two youngest children or grandchildren travelled to exciting new parts of the world, or on the many cruises that we took, I got that 'happiness' kick which I so craved. It was the only emotion that I had carried with me for so many years. (After my Dad died of Heart disease in 1990, amazingly, with the history surrounding him, I couldn't cry, under any circumstances, for twenty years! His death has been the biggest single event in my life so far, emotionally. WHY?) As a Property Manager for over twenty years, in charge of looking after millions of dollars' worth of property, I felt important, full of responsibility, on which I thrived, and it was this which met my needs of being 'wanted', something that I had always needed since I had been the eldest of the six Walsh children. That I changed both houses and jobs (and countries!) to such an extent, tells of my constant need for change, excitement, and something new to look forward to. I was never to be happy and settled, and I was always

CRY

looking for the next 'fix'. As I said, it was in the later years, that I found some short-lived happiness in planning, booking and then going, on holidays. When I worked for Yellow Pages in Canberra, I did so well (I always had to excel at everything I did. I liked the admiration it brought with it!) that I won a two-week trip for Mike and I to Hawaii. I earned so much money that year, that once Hawaii was over, we took our two youngest children (whom I'd also paid to come with us to Hawaii) over to Paris and England. After I became an Author, the Royalty cheques would pay for those numerous Cruises to the South Pacific Islands, or the Top End of Australia, or to fly to Dubai, Hong Kong, a Coach Tour of Italy, a long holiday in England (where I visited Agatha Christie's house 'Greenway' in Devon). The only way I had to stay happy was to constantly have something to look forward to and I would often book Mike, Julia and I four holidays a year, for a number of years towards the end of our marriage. But soon, the gloss had to come off. I realized that no amount of travelling and holidays (I wasn't interested in material things, although many years ago I did get pleasure out of collecting antiques – furniture and Royal Doulton plates and figurines) and I looked upon my life as always having been basically meaningless. My self-worth was zero, even though I had put on the façade of the 'strong and capable woman', but really, I was just a very lonely and unhappy one, caught in a marriage I had been too afraid to leave.

TRISH OLLMAN

My children, after being sent to private Catholic schools which we couldn't really afford, as there were four of them, (I was determined to give them the best start in life that I could), have all turned out better than I could have ever hoped. When they were growing up, I tried really hard to be a good mother to them, better than my own mother had been to me and my siblings, and there was no way they were going to have the memory when they were adults of having had a horrible, mean, mother and an unhappy childhood. For the kids, as with me, Mike was never really ever there. Sure, he was there in person, going to work and coming home, and it's to his credit that he never turned to drink or women (Mike and women???) but our children have little or no memory of him being a big part of their lives. (Perhaps Stuart, who shared a love of computers with Mike, may have had some kind of connection with him, as a teenager, as they would both sit at the old Commodore computer and work out how to 'play' with it.) Only my daughter, Shelby, our youngest child, has a very distinct memory of him, but it's not a good one. She remembers bringing a friend home from school when she was around 13 or 14, one day when we lived in York, England. Unfortunately, she walked in on Mike watching 'Girl on Girl' Lesbian Porn on a video tape. When I came home from work and Shelby told me about it and how embarrassed she'd been, (the two girls on the screen had been naked and engaging in sex acts) I took the tape and smashed it with a hammer, telling Mike to take our caravan and go and live in the Caravan Park nearby.

CRY

Before he left, Shelby remembers a very angry Mike yelling at her for telling me. (So he DID have a voice box after all!) She is still affected by that image to this day! He was gone for two days before he came crawling back. And I LET him!!! And still his emotional abuse, (as that's what I know it to have been) continued. My three boys all have good jobs, ones that they enjoy and get paid well for. They have never been in trouble with the Law or been alcoholics, so I'm hoping I've done a good enough job with them. I see two of them regularly, along with my grandchildren. As you know, my youngest boy, Leo, has bought and old farmhouse in Italy. He comes back to Australia to work in the open-face Coal Mines up in northern Queensland in order to earn the money to put a new roof on the two-hundred-year old farmhouse. But with the Covid Pandemic we have, as I write (2020) in the World, who knows when he will be able to return to Italy and make his house into the self-sufficient home of his dreams. Who even knows where he is, or what he's done? He was never the type of boy/man to get into trouble. He is quiet and reserved, an 'old soul' who loves his wind-up gramophone and old records, dressing beautifully and taking care of himself. Polite and well-meaning. That is the Leo that I last spoke to in December 2019. Where is he now? Will I ever see him again? Something tells me, probably not!

After finally leaving Mike, and my precious Julia, who chose (WHY?) to stay with him (he had been waiting on her 'hand and foot' for years, while I, the Big Bad

Wolf, had insisted on the 16-year old performing just ONE household chore a week in order to 'earn' her $50 weekly pocket money, she didn't like that and anyway, Mike, as pathetic as ever, would do the chore for her before she even had time to think about doing it!) He made her incredibly lazy, something I had hoped to avoid. But when she was 17, she had been in the local Air Cadets for about a year, and suddenly announced that she wanted to join the RAAF (after visiting Williamstown Air Base with the Cadets, she had fallen in love with the planes and the Air Force ethos. She made a formal application to join as 'Ground Crew' and took the Entrance Exam. She was to get an amazing 98% in the test, one of the highest ever. Her knowledge of the RAAF and the planes was exceptional. I might just add here, that for about 18 months after I left home, Julia, the light of my life, had not spoken to me, preferring to give her loyalties to Mike (again WHY?) This broke my heart. The few times she had spoken to me, she always wanted something. One time it was my BMW. I said no, so she stopped speaking to me again. I was to miss out on all her Cadet parades and ceremonies as to her, I was 'persona non gratis'. James, having served almost a year in Detention, was sent by Social Services to live in Sydney, a good four hours away. He would ring me every single day, every time saying he wanted to come back to Queanbeyan to live and to be with me. Now, there was no way I was having him live with me. His anger and temper would mean that I wouldn't be able to sleep at night. But I fought FACS (Social Services)

CRY

for nine long, hard months, even going as high as the Minister, and eventually taking them to Court, to get James back to Queanbeyan. Eventually, not long ago, I was successful (I found out that at age 17, he was old enough to leave FACS care of his own accord, as long as he was safe. So one day, he just he packed his things and moved back home, As Mike had a spare room, for the moment I got him to agree to have James for a while. But with Julia, with whom he had had a deep-rooted jealousy of, also living there, disaster was bound to happen, and it did. James had to be hauled away by the police and taken back into care. Unfortunately, we were to find out that he has been taking drugs and alcohol for some time. The future for poor James doesn't look rosy at this time, as I really don't think that there is anything (I tried for months!) that can help him. Where he goes from here (he's 18 next year (2021) and completely on his own) I just don't know.

Having obtained the Unit that I now live in. I've bought bits and pieces of furniture, ornaments etc. and taken all of my Royal Doulton and china from Mike and now have a lovely home in which to live. I have decided that I will always be better off on my own and no longer search for another man to come into my life. I am excited and keen to start writing my next book, 'The Naked Housewife' a raunchy tale of two single mums who start their own business cleaning in just skimpy underwear and an apron. (That's all you're getting! Lol)

TRISH OLLMAN

After a few false starts, and as I write, Julia and I are back to our old selves, with me worshiping her just as much now as the day she was born, and, it appears, she me. She now stays over on weeknights, going back to her room as Mikes to spend time with her dog, Angus. I enjoy looking after her and she has turned out to a beautiful young woman with her head screwed on. Because Of the Covid Pandemic, now in 2020, her RAAF intake to do her Basic Training, was put off until October. Undeterred, Julia decided to go back to College and get a better ATAR Score as she has decided that she now wants to become a RAAF Officer. She'll make it, of that I have no doubt. She passed her driving test last year and drives herself everywhere, doesn't drink, smoke or take drugs, and I couldn't be prouder of her. I do have a suspicion that she has some loyalty to Mike and it is something that I have to try and ignore. I don't say anything as I don't want to 'rock the boat' but I am really hurt that she still wants to go back to him at weekends. My other grandchildren, apart from the two youngest, who I adore, I barely ever see. They are all grown up now and are all doing well. While I did have a fair bit to do with them as children, it seems these days that once older, grandchildren want to live their own lives. I can only let them, but they know I'm here if they ever need me. Mark continues to do well. I don't hear from him that often, but our conversations are always happy ones, and I know if I ever need him, he'd be there. Stuart, I see more often. His two youngest love spending time with me and both he and they know I'm always here for them also. Shelby, I see pretty much every day. She lives alone with her two cats, just at the top of my street. The situation between Mike and I is at a Stale-Mate. Sometimes we talk, sometimes we don't. Sometimes we must, for our children's and grandchildren's sake. But I now can look back and see the control he had over me, a mental control which he was able to cover-up with all of his other problems. I'm no longer interested in wanting him to change, to become better and kinder, to me. I just don't want him, full stop. Why oh why did I stay with him for so long? I only wish I knew. Mike, with his fifty or so years of lacking interest in me, his lack of communication, care and attention, to both me and our children, was the cause of our marriage disintegrating. Not only did he use pornography to satisfy that part of his life, but he used it to exclude me, which, although it suited me physically, made me feel unloved and unwanted, and he was to give me no mental or emotional stimulation or encouragement whatsoever. Throughout my life, I have been forced to seek replacements for what was missing from my life, firstly with my Grandma, then with the boys and men I went with, then as an adult, getting married at only 16 to a totally unsuitable boy who turned into a totally unsuitable man, the ever-changing jobs, houses and holidays. As I have said, recently, although now far too late, it was felt by members of the family, and a counsellor friend of mine, that Mike may have always been on the Autistic Spectrum. But that's no excuse. He knew in 1968 that he wasn't normal and had many years to go and seek help, as I often asked him to. He had, and still has, barely no conversation whatsoever, no emotional connection to me, our children, and subsequently, our grandchildren, and has shown no affection or love to anyone, especially me. We will never know, and it is now way too late for us to find out. He may not be Autistic. It may just be his (weird) personality. Who knows? Maybe he was dropped on his head as a baby, as he himself once said. But I'd like to know what bloody stars aligned to bring Mike and I together back in 1967? Who was it, looking down upon us from above, who thought that he and I would ever make a good match? If you can imagine the first 35 or so years of our marriage as me being increasingly frustrated with him, and that frustration getting worse and worse over the years, then about 40 or so years into the marriage, that frustration turning into anger, which lasted for another ten years, is it any wonder that I left Mike, Julia, Hamish and Angus, my dogs, and all of the remnants of my life after fifty years in November 2018, and in a situational rage. Since then, I have, for the first time in my life, lived alone. My children, although now busy with their own lives still show me by their actions that they do love me, and my grandchildren, especially three of them, bring so much joy and happiness into my life. In the past year, I did try to find another 'partner' to share what's left of my life with, but as it has been for the past 55 years, (I'm older now and know how to just say 'NO') as soon as any kind of intimacy is mentioned, I run like a rabbit down a hole. I have recently resigned myself to always

CRY

being alone. As far as I can see, men, as always, and even at my age, will always have just one end result in mind, and I'm afraid it's just not going to happen, just as it's barely happened for the fifty years of our marriage. Fifty years. What a waste of a life of potential happiness. Don't get me wrong. I don't feel sorry for myself, and I hope this book doesn't come across as such. But do you know what, every day, I count my blessings. All of my children and grandchildren are still alive, none of them are in Goal, are alcoholics, or use heavy drugs, (well, apart from James) and they are all fit and well. That must stand for a lot. Plus, I must mention, I've had a great deal of success with my six Books. When writing this book, it obviously was never my intention to show myself as a victim, more as a survivor. I'm hoping I won't be judged. Everything I have written is the truth, but I need you to understand that as adults, we are the products of our earlier lives, our childhoods and those years just as we reach adulthood. Why was I born into the massively dysfunctional and abusive family that I was born into? When I needed love, caring and companionship, at a time in my young life when I was completely broken and abused, why did the stars align and bring Mike and I together? As for what do I think of Mike now? well, you already know that answer to that! And the most important question? Why on earth didn't I leave him years ago? There is no answer. So thanks Mum. Thanks for all your love and affection and for looking after me so well. Thanks, Dad, for teaching me to despise sex, to throw myself at any boy who complimented me, and finally, thanks Mike. Thanks for the fifty years of my life that you wasted. But hey, you know what? My past with both my parents and with you, Mike, have made me into the strong and capable woman I am today and always have been, the successful International Author and Screenwriter that I have become. But as for my life, I can now only CRY for what could have been.

THE END

Printed in Great Britain
by Amazon